—❧❦◆❧❦—

BEYOND THE ANCIENT DOOR

—❧❦◆❧❦—

"Free to Move about the Heavens"

By
JAMES A. DURHAM

www.xulonpress.com

TABLE OF CONTENTS

FOREWARD AND ACKNOWLEDGEMENTS vii

CHAPTER 1: The Vision 9

CHAPTER 2: Venturing into Intimacy with God 28

CHAPTER 3: A Victory in View 55

CHAPTER 4: Called to be Valiant 71

CHAPTER 5: Visitation is Vital 96

CHAPTER 6: Vertical Perspective 122

CHAPTER 7: Vision Released 143

CHAPTER 8: Kingdom Values 167

CHAPTER 9: Turning Up the Volume 188

CHAPTER 10: Becoming Virulent Vegetation. 205

CHAPTER 11: Vocabulary of the Kingdom. 218

CHAPTER 12: Visionaries See and Value 234

SUMMARY 245

AN IMPARTATION 257

FOREWARD AND ACKNOWLEDGEMENTS

I want to make this very simple and straight forward. I only have one acknowledgment for this book. This is the Lord's book. He gave it to me during many Third Heaven visits. He told me to publish it. He gave me the titles and an outline for all twelve chapters. He gave the content by revelation and inspiration. He provided all the information for the conclusion. This is first and last His book.

I want to thank the Lord for allowing me to participate in this great adventure of getting His book down on paper and published.

I pray that you will take no offense at my use of the term "His book." Offense is a weapon of the enemy which he readily uses to block or hinder our learning from the Lord. I pray that the Lord will protect you from every attack during your reading of this book and in your intimate times of visitation with Him.

CHAPTER ONE

THE VISION

The earth is the Lord's, and everything in it, the world, and all who live in it; for he founded it upon the seas and established it upon the waters. Who may ascend the hill of the Lord? Who may stand in his holy place? He who has clean hands and a pure heart, who does not lift up his soul to an idol or swear by what is false. He will receive blessing from the Lord and vindication from God his Savior. Such is the generation of those who seek him, who seek your face, O God of Jacob. (Selah) Lift up your heads, O you gates; be lifted up, you ancient doors, that the King of glory may come in. Who is this King of glory? The Lord strong and mighty, the Lord mighty in battle. Lift up your heads, O you gates; lift them up, you ancient doors, that the King of glory may come in. Who is he, this King of glory? The Lord Almighty—he is the King of glory. (Psalm 24, NIV)

It was an early September morning, and the weather in Texas had already begun to change as signs of fall were progressively being revealed by the surroundings. It had been a very hot summer with over two months of temperatures going well beyond 100 degrees. Most of the vegetation had lost its rich green appearance months earlier and now seemed to be crying out as if from a great thirst. This was the third year of draught and some "gloom and doom" voices were speaking of famine. In times like these, God chooses to speak words of hope and restoration to His people. In times like these, people are ready to listen and have leaned heavenward for a word from the Lord.

It was on a morning like this, as I worshipped and prayed for wisdom and revelation, that God gave me a lengthy open vision. I was literally translated in the Spirit to the Secret Place of the Most High God. It was an amazing experience and came to me in what I started to call an Ultra HD vision. Along with the very amazing things I was shown, I was also given specific instructions for understanding and implementing this message from the Lord.

In this vision from the Lord, I clearly saw the hideous face of our ancient enemy (Satan or the devil). He had a greenish color around the whites of his eyes and the pupils were red like fire. His fierce look made no attempt to hide his intentions, which are clearly stated by Jesus in the tenth chapter of the book of John.

> *"The thief does not come except to steal, and to kill, and to destroy."* (John 10:10a)

With this very unpleasant beginning to the vision, I was unsure where it would go from that point forward. So I immediately spoke a prayer of submission to God and asserted my resistance to the enemy. I used a prayer derived from:

> *"Therefore submit to God. Resist the devil and he will flee from you."* (James 4:7)

I have converted this Biblical passage into a prayer I use daily. My daily prayer follows:

"Father God, I submit to you in spirit, soul, and body; all that I am and all that I ever will be. All that I have and all that I ever will have I submit to you! I resist the devil, and in accordance with your word and in the mighty name of Jesus, he has no choice but to flee and take all his works with him, in Jesus' mighty name! Amen and Amen!"

After this short prayer, I asked the Lord to rebuke the enemy on my behalf and he immediately disappeared. Thank God that the power of His Word never diminishes and never becomes ineffective!

Behind the place where the enemy had stood, I was shown an ancient, arched door. It was aged and weathered, but even the large cracks in the wood had not weakened it. The wooden frame that arched around the door was not smooth from sanding, but roughly hewn with ancient tools. Time, wear, and weather had softened the edges of the marks left by chisels and saws. In spite of age and wear, the wood in the door looked almost new. It had the appearance of the wood on a freshly refurbished wooden deck. The color was sandy brown with a reddish hue and seemed to have some type of weather-proofing smoothly and expertly applied to protect the finish. I immediately thought it must be gopher wood to have endured all the centuries and still be so strong. There was something strange about this door. It had large, thick, and imposing bronze hinges on both sides. There was no visible handle or door knob. By human wisdom and knowledge, there seemed to be no way to open the door.

As I observed the door with amazement and fascination, it faded behind clouds which came across the front like smoke from a wildfire. I knew there was a revelation behind the door, and I was certain that this was another attempt by the enemy to prevent me from receiving this message from the Lord. So I pressed in with all my spirit in order to see the door again. Three times I prayerfully asked the Holy Spirit to help me understand the meaning of the door.

In response to my prayers, the clouds cleared and I was able to see the door again. This time I saw that the challenge of opening the door was greater than I had first noticed. In addition to having such imposing hinges on both sides, vines had grown over the lower and middle parts of the door.

As I contemplated the door and searched for its meaning, I noticed a single rosebud on a very long stem over the top right portion of vines covering the door. It was an old, white rosebud that had never opened. The edges of the petals had begun to turn brown with decay. There were no leaves on the long stem of the rose. It was producing nothing and it was clear to me that it was near death.

I asked the Holy Spirit what this rosebud meant. I was told that it represented the visible church. Its mission has always been to open and close the door at the direction of the Holy Spirit, but it has never fully opened up in order to be led and empowered for its purpose in the kingdom of God. I was told by the Spirit that if it doesn't open up soon to the fullness of its purpose, it will continue to decay and eventually die. This was a very sobering thought which I began to ponder in my heart.

As I attempted to fully understand this message and to grasp it with my natural mind, the door suddenly swung wide open, seemingly by itself. I received by revelation knowledge that the Holy Spirit was doing the work which had originally been assigned to the church, and it was He who had opened the door for me.

As I looked through the open door, I realized for the first time that the door opened into a very large tree. I began to hear spoken words and I heard myself saying them out loud: "An oak of righteousness! An oak of righteousness! An oak of righteousness!" At this point, Isaiah 61:3 came to mind: *"They will be called oaks of righteousness, a planting of the Lord for the display of his splendor,"* (NIV). It became clear that the creator of this tree, door, and opening was none other than Father God Himself. It also became clear that its purpose was to display the splendor of the Lord.

As I began to confess that this was the work of God, I was

allowed to enter with the invitation: "Enter now into the secret place of the Most High!" I heard this three times and spoke it three times. Later, I was led to three scriptures to more fully understand the meaning of what I was now experiencing.

> *"He who dwells in the secret place of the Most High shall abide under the shadow of the Almighty."* (Psalm 91:1)

> *"You shall hide them in the secret place of Your presence from the plots of man; You shall keep them secretly in a pavilion from the strife of tongues."* (Psalm 31:20)

> *"But you, when you pray, go into your room, and when you have shut your door, pray to your Father who is in the secret place; and your Father who sees in secret will reward you openly."* (Matthew 6:6)

I received by revelation-knowledge what God intended by showing this door. It is God's desire for us to enter into His secret place and to fellowship with Him. He is not content for us to be shut out or prevented from being in His presence. He doesn't want us to avoid His presence. He wants to set us free from the spirit of fear, which brings judgment and condemnation. It is His desire for us to have a place in the Spirit where we can experience His presence and protection, His goodness is His glory, and He wants to reveal that goodness to each of us as a guarantee of His grace. He wants us to spend time with Him. For this reason, He has removed every roadblock. Jesus has provided a garment of praise like the linen garments the priest wore when he ministered in the Holy of Holies. This is why Jesus declared His purpose so early in His ministry by reading from Isaiah 61:

> *"The Spirit of the Sovereign LORD is on me, because the LORD has anointed me to preach good news to the poor. He has sent me to bind up the brokenhearted, to proclaim freedom for the captives and release from darkness for the prisoners, to proclaim the year of the LORD's favor and the day of vengeance of our God, to comfort all who mourn, and provide for those who grieve in Zion—to bestow on them a crown of beauty instead of ashes, the oil of gladness instead of mourning, and a garment of praise instead of a spirit of despair. They will be called oaks of righteousness, a planting of the LORD for the display of his splendor."* (Isaiah 61:1-3, NIV)

Jesus has provided the blood of the sacrifice, which is required as a covering over sinful human beings who want to enter into God's presence. Our prayers lifted up to the Father in the Spirit are our equivalent of the smoke from incense burning on the golden altar. God has provided all we need. Now the invitation has been sent forth, and the decision is ours.

When I was fully inside the "Secret Place of the Most High," I saw a chair that was elevated on a platform near the back of the room. At first, I thought this was a place to enter, sit down, and be refreshed. But it was revealed to me that this was the throne of the Lord. As I looked at the chair, a cloud began to fill the room. I was partially in the cloud. It filled the room and rose over my feet and partially up my calves. The cloud slowly moved upward and occupied the seat. Then it filled the room. In spite of the weighty presence of the Lord and the thickness of the cloud, it did not block my view.

As I watched these things unfold before my eyes, I began to receive very specific instruction in my spirit. This was what Jesus had meant when He said that the Holy Spirit would teach us and guide us into all truth. In my spirit, I clearly heard the

Lord say, "*The glory of the Lord fills the Secret Place where He calls us to dwell with Him.*" This reminded me of the promise released in Psalm 91:1. Unfortunately, many people in the church (like Israel at Sinai) do not want to go into the cloud because of their fear. They fear the Lord will destroy them because of their iniquity. In my spirit, I wanted to cry out to them, "But the Glory of the Lord is wonderful." The purplish/blue flame of His glory danced around me and enveloped me. I cannot adequately describe how wonderful this experience was except to say that it was totally awesome.

I felt so content to be in this place, but I was admonished, "This is not the stopping place." My spirit was informed that disciples keep making the same mistake. We want to build tents on the Mount of Transfiguration rather than being enlightened by listening to the Word. On the mountain, the voice of the Lord instructed Peter, James and John, "*This is My beloved Son, in whom I am well pleased. Hear Him!*" (Matthew 17:5) The hearing part is the problem, because so many people simply do not want to do what He says.

Even as I received this admonishment, I felt a growing holy-hunger for more of Him and to move from glory to glory into the image He has for me. So I prayed intently (aloud): "Holy Spirit, teach me! Holy Spirit, teach me! Holy Spirit, teach me!"

As soon as this prayer was spoken, I was moved outside again. This sudden experience of being moved back outside was something like a film being re-wound. Everything moved in reverse. I had no control over this movement. This was a very surprising experience and I was in shock. My thoughts went wild. I thought that perhaps I had said something wrong. I feared that the experience was over, and there was so much more that I wanted to learn. And more than this, I didn't want to lose that awesome feeling of being so content and at peace in His presence. As I wrestled and agonized with these thoughts, the Holy Spirit resumed my instruction and I quickly learned why this had happened. I was taken outside again where I could be taught the process for getting into the secret place of the Most High.

I learned that as we open up our spirits to the Holy Spirit and allow Him to instruct us, the righteousness of Christ opens the door. He is the only one worthy to open the door. All of our efforts to make it happen are futile. We need to be in Christ for the door to open to the "secret place of the Most High God."

The church as a whole has looked at the door and assumed that it's the door in Revelation 3:20. Many believers think they are on the inside and Jesus is on the outside asking to come in. The church of the past has thought it was in control of the door and could allow as much of Christ in as would make the people comfortable. Most Christians have accepted this level of religious experience and have not hungered for more. This was revealed in the mystery of the rose. The church has attempted to keep God under control in order to limit His demands on their daily living. Most believers have wanted just enough of Christ to get saved, but not enough to place kingdom demands on their lives.

But I was taught by the Holy Spirit that we are not seeing the door correctly. The truth is that we're on the outside being invited in. If you don't understand which side of the door you're on, you will not be able to pass through the door. If you don't understand who is really in control, you will be like the wilted rosebud, never reaching your potential. If you're not ready to move through the door, you are doomed to waste away in limited usefulness. So what should we choose? I remembered Joshua's challenge to the people of Israel:

> *"And if it seems evil to you to serve the Lord, choose for yourselves this day whom you will serve, whether the gods which your fathers served that were on the other side of the River, or the gods of the Amorites, in whose land you dwell. But as for me and my house, we will serve the Lord."*
> (Joshua 24:15)

I made my choice. Like Joshua, as for me and my house, we will always choose to serve the Lord! Amen? Pause for a moment and make your decision. It is critical to choose before moving forward in your quest for Third Heaven visitation.

When I came to understand these teachings, the door opened again and I was allowed to move back inside. I found myself in a kneeling position before the throne. I knew clearly who was in charge. I knew that I was the humble servant who had been invited into the very presence of the Most High God. I knew that it was not because of my virtue or accomplishments, but because of what Christ had done. This was not a humiliating or belittling kind of experience. This spoke to me of a holy privilege given to undeserving people because God loves us. It was and is an experience of love beyond human understanding. In the Secret Place there is an overwhelming sense of the Lord's warm welcome. It is an experience of being wanted, loved, and cared for by the most important Person who has ever existed. Again, I felt uplifted by my knowledge that this is a holy privilege and a sacred trust.

As I bowed and worshiped the Lord, I noticed an ornate sword mounted on the wall of the tree to my left and to the right side of the throne. I like swords and I liked seeing the sword of the Lord prominently displayed on the wall. In my spirit, I thought, "That's nice!"

I was immediately corrected with these words, "That is not nice! That is not where the Sword of the Lord is supposed to be! It is not a decoration for you to display in your homes or churches. It is the living Word of God. Where should the sword be?" I knew the answer and responded, "It's supposed to be in my heart." Suddenly, the sword was no longer visible on the wall, and I knew that it had moved to where it was supposed to be. It was now in my heart. The sting of this correction was immediately removed as I felt the awesome presence of the Word of the Lord in my heart. That was and is a very comforting feeling.

I repeated this prayer out loud three times. "Holy Spirit, teach me! Holy Spirit, guide me into all truth! Holy Spirit, please tell me what Heaven is saying today!"

As I completed this prayer, I saw a heart. It was not a picture or a valentine type of red heart. It was a real, living, human heart like you see in medical books or training films for health-care professionals. The arteries were cut and the ends open, and yet it was very much alive. The heart moved into a position over the center of the throne. I heard the Spirit say, "The Lord is replacing old hearts with new ones." God's Word never changes. His promises are never lost. What He has been doing in the past, He is doing now. And He will continue to do His work on Earth until the end of time. That is good news, and it is very reassuring.

As I pondered and celebrated this promise, something was visually displayed before me. The word "HOPE," written in a giant script, appeared over the throne. It was quickly replaced by the word "HABITATION," which also moved into a position over the throne. Three times I repeated, "Heart, Hope, Habitation!" as I prayed "Holy Spirit, help me to remember these things."

In response to this prayer, I was taught by the Spirit that it is God's plan to give us new hearts (spirits), a living hope, and to dwell with us. However, this can't happen until we're willing to let the Spirit lead us into the "Secret Place." And we will not be able to be led into the secret place until we truly allow the Holy Spirit to guide us into "all truth." Further, we will not be led into all truth until we're willing to let God be the director of our lives. And, finally, we will not have God as the true director of our lives until we're willing to spend quality time with Him in the "Secret Place." This sounds circular in logic, but don't get bogged down in mental exercises. Instead, trust the Holy Spirit—who fully understands this—to guide you through the entire process.

Spending quality time with God must go beyond mere

willingness to give Him an hour on Sunday or a quick prayer at meal time. Spending quality time with God must become the top priority in our lives if we expect to have Him dwelling with us. That time we commit to spending with Him needs to be so fixed that even our day planners have permanent times set aside for Him which will not be replaced by any lesser things which may come up. This time with the Father is as critical to survival in the spirit as breathing is to the survival of our bodies. The body was created to automatically breathe without our conscious control. However, breathing in the spirit is a learned response and is only possible with continual dedication, focus, and concentration.

> *"So Jesus said to them again, 'Peace to you! As the Father has sent Me, I also send you.' And when He had said this, He breathed on them, and said to them, 'Receive the Holy Spirit.'"* (John 20:21-22)

Jesus breathed the Spirit on the disciples, and they had to breathe the Spirit into themselves to truly receive Him. We must learn the habit of breathing the Holy Spirit into our spirits. We must become so fixed in our spiritual habit of breathing in the Spirit that it will become as automatic as the body breathing in air.

This became increasingly clear to me as I spent more and more time in the Secret Place. Each time I stood in or bowed down into the cloud of His presence, this need to breathe in the Spirit became more and more established as essential to my survival. In the midst of that cloud, I began to consciously breathe in His Shekinah Glory. It was so warm and reassuring to be so close to Him and to realize that I could literally breathe His presence into my soul. As I continued to do this, I started to remember the stories of the children and youth at the Azusa Street Mission during the revival. They loved to play in the cloud of His presence and breathe in the air of His Shekinah glory. I was doing the same thing, and I was loving and luxuriating in this wonderful experience. It was as if I could breathe in the very life force of God. I felt as if I were being made eternal in the process of breathing this air of His presence. As I continued to enjoy this experience, my eyes were directed upward by the Spirit.

I was surprised by what I saw. I had mistakenly thought I was in a room with a ceiling. However, now I could see that there was a passageway upward. I could now see a staircase just behind the chair where the Lord was seated. I willingly and joyfully allowed the Spirit to move me upward. As I ascended the stairs, I saw that the heavens were open over me. The view was awesome. I looked up into what appeared to be an evening sky. I saw extremely bright stars completely filling a deep blue sky. The blueness of the sky spoke of daytime, while the stars made it appear to be nighttime. It was difficult to determine which was real. Then I realized that both things were true in the spiritual realm. I was still trying to understand it in terms of natural laws. I came to realize that we have to move beyond these limitations to receive all the Lord has for us. As I continued to take all this in, I was in awe of this entire experience of the heavens which was so overwhelmingly beautiful. I was only allowed to reflect on this for a moment, because my spirit shifted to my deep longing to move upward.

I asked, "Holy Spirit, what does this mean? Help me to understand all of these things I am seeing and experiencing!" He responded, "The Father wants His people to move into the Secret Place where they can receive revelation knowledge to prepare them to be taken higher into the realms of His glory."

In the Secret Place, we can move into a position of heavenly provision. We can go to our meeting room with the Father and be equipped to do the work of our calling as well as the ministry tasks of our anointing. However, we must always remember that this is not the stopping place. Like the Mount of Transfiguration, it is a place where we get a brief glimpse of His eternal glory. It is a place where we go in order to have our focus once again directed to and fixed on Jesus. In its full sense, it is an equipping place to prepare the saints for the work of the ministry.

I suddenly realized that the secret place is like a launching pad. From this place, we're equipped and then launched back into the world to do kingdom business. In this place we receive the fuel, the energy, and the mission perimeters for the work He has called us to do for His glory.

For many people, there is a tendency to believe that visions and experiences like this are special times just for our benefit. However, the Spirit reminds us that it is not just about one person. It is shocking to discover that it is not all about me, and it is not all about you. We have to get over ourselves in order to be useful for the work of the Lord. Please understand that visits to the secret place are not times for us to be self-focused and whining, "What about me?"

A few days after this visit to the Secret Place, I had another vision in which I was caught up into the throne room. Millions of angels surrounded the throne of God and were literally glowing with the radiance of God. This radiant glory is imparted to angels and people while they are in His presence. This glory glow continues to increase as we give ourselves totally to Him in worship. This awesome glory, which looked like fire all around Father God, was an awesome and inspiring sight for me. But from where I was seated with Christ in this heavenly place, I began to notice that there was very little light surrounding Him. This seemed very inappropriate. As I thought about this, I was lifted by the Spirit above and moved over the area where the angels were glowing in worship. This gave me a very good view of the area around Jesus. The church, His bride, was gathered around Him, but there was very little worship being offered up. Most of the seats were empty. The Spirit told me that so many of the saints have never occupied their seats in the heavenly place (Ephesians 2:6). Others were looking to themselves and their thoughts were revealed. They were asking, "What about me?" "What about my ministry?" "Will visiting here cause more people to come to my church and follow my teaching?" "How will this help me?" Hearing these thoughts in this place made these people look so dark and so out of place. No wonder the light was dim around Christ. The church is so focused on itself and how it will be elevated that it is incapacitated for the purpose of the pure worship of our Lord Jesus. Some of the saints began to focus on Christ in worship and a faint glow began to emerge around Him. I was convicted and gave Him all the worship I was capable of giving.

When we are in the secret place, it is the time and the place to ask what He wants us to do, and then to be made ready and fully equipped to move out and accomplish the tasks we are given. In the military, soldiers who are given orders move out in order to accomplish their assigned missions. That is also what true disciples do. It is about His glory, His kingdom, His will, and His vision. We are privileged to be allowed to share in His work and to be made fit vessels for His service by the blood of Jesus. We must remember that we didn't earn it and we don't deserve it, but He is so good as to allow us to be a part of His glorious work.

I pray that we will keep our eyes fixed on Jesus! I pray that we will spend more time listening attentively to Him, and then be quick to do what He commissions! As I thought about these things, I remembered what James said about being "doers of the word."

> *"But be doers of the word, and not hearers only, deceiving yourselves. For if anyone is a hearer of the word and not a doer, he is like a man observing his natural face in a mirror; for he observes himself, goes away, and immediately forgets what kind of man he was. But he who looks into the perfect law of liberty and continues in*

it, and is not a forgetful hearer but a doer of the
work, this one will be blessed in what he does."
(James 1:22-25)

I knew that it was about time to leave. I had mixed emotions. I wanted to stay, but I also wanted to be able to go back to my office and write this down.

I was then told by the Spirit to write this vision down and share it with all who would listen. So I asked for Him to keep the remembrance of each detail in my mind. When I receive a powerful vision like this, I often become so caught up in the moment that I forget some of the details unless I write them down immediately. The Holy Spirit was faithful to answer this request. Thanks be to God! He is so faithful!

I also knew in my spirit that this Secret Place is a location to which we can return daily to be fed and equipped to do His work and to continue to accomplish His purpose.

As I pondered this vision over the next two days, I became more and more convinced that there was more to it. Friday morning, as I worshipped, I felt an exceptionally strong presence of the Lord. I asked to see the rest of the vision. I was caught up again in the praise music and found myself asking God to come down in power. These words had barely cleared my mouth, when I distinctly heard from Heaven, **"NO! YOU COME UP HERE!"**

The ancient wooden door stood before me again. Again, it opened to allow me in. I was overjoyed as I was being led inside once again. I was filled with expectancy, because I was sure that more would be revealed and this teaching experience would continue.

I saw that everything inside the "oak of righteousness" was as it had been before. The cloud was there again, and I moved through the cloud that surrounded my feet until it came up almost knee high. I was moved by the Spirit past the wooden chair (His throne in the Secret Place) and up the stairs to the left side of the chair.

As I reached the level where there was an open Heaven, I raised my arms in worship and praise. I heard the Lord say, "My people keep asking me to come down there and fix things. I've already done that. Now, it is time for them to come up here." Then He said with a commanding, yet gentle and loving voice, **"COME UP HERE!"**

Immediately, I was in the throne room standing by my seat. The Throne Room was especially glorious Friday morning. God was being worshipped with great power in Heaven. I clearly saw the 10,000 times 10,000 and thousands of thousands of angels surrounding the throne. They were all glowing like a raging fire as they gave Him wholehearted praise. God's light, energy, power, and life force was flowing everywhere. It was like standing in a huge field of static electricity that was flowing around and through my body.

I found myself face down in the gold dust on the floor of Heaven as I was receiving instruction from the Lord. He said, "Tell my people to come up here! It is time for them to come up and be filled with kingdom authority and kingdom principles. I want them to come here, be filled with the kingdom, and then take it back with them to Earth. They are to take the kingdom to Earth just as my Son did before. Then my kingdom can come on Earth as it is in Heaven, and my will can be done on Earth as it is in Heaven. It's your time to be carriers of the kingdom. But you need to come up to this place and be filled with it so you can go back and release it throughout the world. Now, go back and invite my people to come up here!"

I wish that I could tell you that I took the noble path and said, "Yes Lord! Here am I, send me!" But I have to be honest and tell you that's not what happened. My response was from the flesh. I said, "Lord, are you sure you want me to tell this?" I immediately heard three voices in unity speak a commanding, **"YES!"** It would be nice to be able to say that I responded with an immediate acceptance of this command, but I continued to question the request. I

24

said, "But Lord, ever since you asked me to share visions with people, many of them think I am half crazy. If I do this, they will all be convinced that I am completely crazy!" The Lord said to me, "Oh! And who do you think you are?" Wow! That put it all into perspective. It isn't about me or my reputation. It is about Him and what He has planned for the kingdom. I said, "Yes, Sir!"

Immediately, I saw in my spirit Moses taking that same message to the Hebrews. He told them to consecrate themselves and go up the mountain with him. But they said, "No!" They asked him to go up the mountain, meet with God, and bring His Word back to them. They were afraid because they knew that sinful people cannot live in the presence of God. God made a way, but they made an excuse. God opened the door, and they sent Moses through it. In my spirit, I wondered what they missed by turning down the offer to hear directly from God. What would their story have been like if they had said, "Yes!" to God's invitation?

Then a big question came into my mind: "Will we make the same mistake?" I realized in that moment that many will choose not to change, and there is nothing I can do about that. However, I can do something about my decision. And you can do something about your decision. Will you respond to the Lord's invitation and ascend into His presence? Will you allow Him to fill you with the kingdom and transform you into a kingdom carrier? Are there any volunteers to be kingdom carriers? Will you become a transformer for the Lord?

My mission from the Lord on the following Sunday was to impart Third Heaven visitation to those attending the service. I was told to use oil to anoint those who were willing to travel to God's Secret Place and be equipped to carry the kingdom. Additionally, I was told to insist that they think this through very carefully. This is a huge commitment. You and I should not do it unless we are truly willing to be ambassadors for His kingdom. Are you ready to make that vow?

It is a matter of making an unbreakable vow. I did as I was told and anointed all who were willing with an oil of freedom. I then laid hands on those willing to receive this impartation and spoke the words of the Lord over them. The Lord assured me that this would impart authority to them to find and enter His secret place. It was very important to me that all present take communion over it before receiving the impartation. I understood this to be a blood covenant with the Lord, and I asked them to enter the same agreement with the Lord.

I was told to assure all believers who were willing to listen that God wants them to meet Him in the secret place so that He can equip them to do kingdom business on Earth.

It would be nice to tell you that I took the high ground and simply obeyed. However, I knew that a particular person was going to be present who had a huge issue about messages like this. So I asked the Lord if He was sure it was to be done on this particular Sunday and not some other time. I immediately heard a resounding, three-voice response, **"YES!"** Then the Lord asked me, "Do you think that a particular person being there is not a part of my plan?" I knew that God is never surprised. He never says, "Wow! I didn't see that coming!" Of course it was part of His plan. It is not up to me to decide who will and who will not hear this vision. So I am trusting God to decide who, what, when and where. It is my task to be obedient and pass on what I have received from Him.

Recently, I have heard and read from many sources that we are to be doing kingdom business. I have listened to the call to conquer the seven mountains of culture. I have been told that we are to use a new vocabulary and speak kingdom principles into the Earth. However, I have not been told by anyone how we are individually to get specific instructions for our part in this process or how we are to understand the principles related to our specific, individual tasks.

We tend to build systems and programs in hopes that we can make the kingdom come on Earth as it is in Heaven. Two thousand years of religious programming and human wisdom have not produced the results called for by Jesus. I am reminded of what the Lord told Zechariah to announce:

> *"'Not by might nor by power, but by My Spirit,'*
> *says the LORD of hosts." (Zechariah 4:6)*

Over the next few weeks, God continued to download these principles to me. This went from a stand-alone message to a sermon series, and finally to a book. My prayer is that the chapters that follow will be something of a guide for you as you enter into your own Secret Place and receive kingdom authority and kingdom principles for yourself. I pray that the Holy Spirit will lead you as He has led me and that you will share with others the additional insights which are given to you.

PRAYER

"For this reason I kneel before you, Father, from whom your whole family in Heaven and on Earth derives its name. I pray that out of your glorious riches you may strengthen me with power through your Spirit in my inner being, so that Christ may dwell in my heart through faith. And I pray that—being rooted and established in love—I may have power, together with all the saints, to grasp how wide and long and high and deep is the love of Christ, and to know this love that surpasses knowledge. I pray that I may be filled to the measure of all your fullness. Now, Father, I know that you are able to do immeasurably more than all I ask or imagine, according to your power that is at work within me. To you be glory in the church and in Christ Jesus throughout all generations, forever and ever! Amen." (Ephesians 3:14-19, NIV, paraphrased to put it in the first person)

CHAPTER 2

VENTURING INTO INTIMACY WITH GOD

A t this point, let me recommend that you read all scripture references aloud. Take note of the advice given in Romans 10:17, "*So then faith comes by hearing, and hearing by the word of God.*" Reading aloud has at least four important benefits.

1. First, when you read aloud, you are confessing with your mouth what God says;

   "For it is with your heart that you believe and are justified, and it is with your mouth that you confess and are saved." (Romans 10:10, NIV)

2. Next, when you read aloud, you hear the voice you trust most (your own) speak aloud the truth of God's Word.

3. Then, when you read aloud, the words you speak are stored in your heart and come forth later as the "good treasure" of your heart.

   "A good man out of the good treasure of his heart brings forth good; and an evil man out of the evil treasure of his heart brings forth evil. For out of the abundance of the heart his mouth speaks." (Luke 6:45)

4. Finally, when you read aloud, you increase your understanding by processing the text with more than one of your five senses (seeing, speaking and hearing).

So, with this understanding, read aloud Psalm 100.

"Shout for joy to the LORD, all the earth. Worship the LORD with gladness; come before him with joyful songs. Know that the LORD is God. It is he who made us, and we are his; we are his people, the sheep of his pasture. Enter his gates with thanksgiving and his courts with praise; give thanks to him and praise his name. For the LORD is good and his love endures forever; his faithfulness continues through all generations." (Psalm 100, NIV)

God is making it clear through scriptures and by the revelations He is giving through His prophets that His heart's desire is to develop an intimate relationship with each and every one of us. It is out of this heart desire of the Father to communicate with His children that access to the Secret Place is made available. Your Father God is inviting you to join Him in this place of intimacy so He can give you gifts, knowledge, understanding, counsel, revelation, and inspiration. He is doing all of this to equip you for the ministry to which He has called you. He has not left you alone without resources. He never will!

During more than 29 years of service as an active duty army chaplain, I was required to go into many "secret places." In order to control who is allowed into these secret places, there is an access roster with the names of those persons with proper security clearances, a need to know, and an invitation to attend.

When you arrive at one of these secret places, you must go through the person charged with controlling access. If your name is in the book, you are allowed in. If your name is not in the book, you are denied access until your security clearance is verified and your need to know is established.

During a time of war, everyone has to leave their cell phones outside the secure room. While in the secret place, you cannot contact anyone outside of the room, including your boss, co-workers, or subordinates. These controls are necessary in order to prevent secrets from getting out to unauthorized agents who might attempt to jeopardize an operation and put those involved in carrying out the mission at risk.

During one period of time with regularly scheduled meetings in the secret place, the security staff realized that people had other types of recording devices. As a result, each person attending had to leave all PDAs, BlackBerrys, cell phones, and digital recorders outside the room under the control of the person maintaining the access roster. These processes and procedures which I learned from the military gave me an interesting revelation about going into the Secret Place of the Most High. We need to let go of all worldly ties during the time we are in His presence. We must let go of the phone lines. We must let go of the recording devices. We must let go of all the ways we stay in contact with the outside world, because we are going into His Secret Place where 100% of our focus and attention must be on Him.

One key to understanding how we gain access to His Secret Place is found in chapter two of the book of Ephesians.

> *"And He came and preached peace to you who were afar off and to those who were near. For through Him we both have access by one Spirit to the Father. Now, therefore, you are no longer strangers and foreigners, but fellow citizens with the saints and members of the household of God, having been built on the foundation of the apostles and prophets, Jesus Christ Himself being the chief cornerstone, in whom the whole building,*

> *being fitted together, grows into a holy temple in*
> *the Lord, in whom you also are being built to-*
> *gether for a dwelling place of God in the Spirit."*
> (Ephesians 2:17-22)

Jesus opened access to the Father not only for Himself, but for us as well. Notice: This is the most important scriptural basis for your authority to enter into God's presence. Paul says that we have been made "members of the household of God" as well as "fellow citizens" in His kingdom. Our citizenship and our family membership together provide us with ample Biblical authority for entering the Secret Place of the Most High. The Holy Spirit is identified as the access officer controlling who will and who will not be allowed to enter.

It is one thing to know that you have access, but it is another thing to know how to find this place of intimacy with God. Where is it located? How do you get there? I will use another military experience to demonstrate this principle.

After the war on terror was under way, we started having meetings very early in the morning, at noon time, and again in the evening. At each meeting, we were given tasks which had to be accomplished before the next meeting. This was a huge challenge since you couldn't write them down; you couldn't record them, and you couldn't put then on your PDA or text it to yourself. You had to remember the details of each request and be certain to accomplish every detail of each assigned task.

Soon, another difficulty emerged. The location of the "secret place" started to change frequently. Attendees would be notified that the regular meeting place was not available and a new location in another command headquarters was to be used. At first I replied, "That's interesting. Where is it located?" Many times, the answer was, "I don't know." So I had to go to the general area and begin looking for the "secret place." At times this was very challenging and no one was available to guide or direct me to the proper place. During these meetings, we were

31

likely to be told that the next meeting was to be conducted at another location in a different headquarters. The challenge was, "Go find it." For security purposes, the meeting places continued to be changed from one location to another on a regular basis.

In a similar manner, we are challenged to find the location of the Secret Place of the Most High. Just as in the military, the location of that place may change from time to time. The challenge is to regularly search for and find that special place of intimacy with God. For me, the initial meeting place was just beyond the ancient door which I described in Chapter One. After a short period of time, the location changed, and it has continued to change from season to season. For you, there may be some completely different location or method of getting into your secret place. In other words, don't try to go to my place or someone else's meeting place. Find your own place for meeting with God and be continually ready for that place to change from time to time. Don't be surprised by changes. Our God is constantly making all things new. Trust Him to reveal what you need to know when you need to know it. An important truth to remember is that it doesn't really matter what someone else has experienced. You cannot duplicate their experience. However, it is critically important that you find your own special place of intimacy with God which is unique to you.

So how do you find that place? I have some good news for you. By the inspiration of the Holy Spirit, the psalmist gave us a detailed plan for approaching the Lord. The approach was revealed in the structure of the temple. David, a man after God's own heart, was a frequent visitor to the Secret Place of the Most High; in other words, to his special place of intimacy with God. Spending time in the secret place was a well developed habit in David's life. I think that is why God called him "a man after my own heart." David loved God and wanted to spend time with his Lord. And Father God loved David, and also wanted to spend time with him. It is this mutual desire of the heart which opens the pathway, and it is the Holy Spirit who leads the way.

In one of those times of intimacy, David revealed that He wanted to build a temple to honor God. However, God did not allow him to build it. He had to let his son Solomon build the temple. However, the Lord respected David's desire and the pure motives behind his request. As a result, God gave David a very detailed plan for the construction of the Temple and all of its furnishings. I believe that as God revealed the Temple plan to David, He also gave him a vision for how we are to approach the Secret Place. This scriptural method of approaching the Lord is imbedded in the directions for approaching Him in the temple. David gives us a detailed description of this process in Psalm 100.

Today we hear many people teaching and singing about rebuilding David's fallen tent.

> *"'After this I will return and rebuild David's fallen tent. Its ruins I will rebuild, and I will restore it, that the remnant of men may seek the Lord and all the Gentiles who bear my name,' says the Lord, who does these things."* (Acts 15:16-17, NIV)

This promise is not about rebuilding the temple. David didn't build the Temple. He constructed a tent in Jerusalem to hold the Ark of Testimony. The message in this prophecy is that God's presence is not to be hidden away in a part of the Temple where only one man has access to God once a year. God wants a place where each of us can draw near every day to give Him thanksgiving, praise, and worship. David's tent gave much greater access to the people than either the Tabernacle or the Temple. Here, in David's tent, worship was offered 24 hours a day, seven days a week. This is the intimacy that God desires to restore with His people. Solomon established the same order of worship in the Temple, but dividing walls of separation were firmly established in the structure and the practice of worship. David's tent allowed greater access and thereby greater and expanded opportunities for intimacy with God.

Here is an important truth: You can't just rush into the presence of God, proclaim that you don't have much time for Him, lay out a list of tasks for His day, and then rush out to your daily activities. Many times this is what our prayer time appears to be. Many people see times of prayer as an opportunity to let God know what they expect of Him without wasting a lot of precious time in the process. But I want to make this clear: the almighty creator God is not the servant of any one of us or all of us combined. He is God, and we are His servants. This order of things needs to be clearly understood so that we can give Him the honor He is due.

We don't have a Santa Claus Jesus who has the task of preparing and delivering presents on our timetable. We have a Savior and Lord. If He is the Lord of our lives, then we serve Him. He doesn't run our errands for us or fix all the broken things in our lives. He gives us the ability to do that. He gives us the authority to do that. He gives us the strength and the power required to accomplish our assigned tasks, and we are expected to do the work.

God wants to have an intimate relationship with us, and in that relationship we find that we are not a group of unhappy servants or miserable slaves. Serving Him is not an odious or painful servitude. We discover that—out of an intimate relationship with Him—we are joyful servants, because we have a gracious God whose glory is His goodness. Remember when Moses asked to see God's glory.

> *"Then He said, I will make all My goodness pass before you, and I will proclaim the name of the Lord before you. I will be gracious to whom I will be gracious, and I will have compassion on whom I will have compassion."* (Exodus 33:19-20)

God's glory is His goodness, and He wants to show all that awesome goodness in our lives. Like Moses, when we see His glory, we too discover that we are the joyful servants of a God who glories in His goodness. In intimacy with Him, we find that what we desire most is to be more like Him every day. This is how we will truly feel in the depths of our hearts, because we have fallen in love with Him. Remember what it was like when you experienced that youthful infatuation for the first time. You wanted to spend all your time with the object of your affection. You thought about him/her all the time, and both of you tried to figure out ways to please one another. Try as you might, you simply couldn't find enough ways to please and enjoy each other.

Sometimes we lose the intensity of these feelings after we get married. We must learn that, to keep our marriage strong, we need to work to keep those feelings alive and active. We have to keep that passion and focus on our marriage partner for those feelings to stay vibrant and alive with romance and commitment. If you want the relationship to last, you have to feed it. It is the same in our relationship with God. We want to fall in love with God over again every day. Every day, we want to do more to please Him and become more and more like Him. We want to become deeply in love with the "lover of our souls." You see, it is all about love. That is the nature of an intimate relationship.

Under the inspiration of the Holy Spirit, God gave a model to Paul. He taught Paul that an ideal marriage relationship is a good model for our relationships with Jesus and with the Father. It is in the falling in love, the intense infatuation, and the staying in love that a marriage is established, stands firm, and grows. God wants us to relate to Him in the very same way. He created this pattern for our marital lives, and He wants us to experience an even more intense and ever-increasing love for Him. When we relate to Him this way, it is truly beautiful. Paul also used this imagery of marriage to help his readers understand better their relationship with the Lord.

"For this reason a man will leave his father and mother and be united to his wife, and the two will become one flesh. This is a profound mystery— but I am talking about Christ and the church. However, each one of you also must love his wife as he loves himself, and the wife must respect her husband." (Ephesians 5:31-33, NIV)

If you want to enter God's presence, you have to do it the right way. It is like those times of military service when I went into the secret places. You can't just barge in where the high ranking officials are located. There is a protocol. There is a process. There is a procedure. You don't just bombard your way in. It is the same when you prepare to enter the Secret Place of the Most High.

You need to learn and practice kingdom protocol and show kingdom etiquette. Follow the pattern established in the Psalms. Begin with the songs of ascent. Psalm 120-138 were sung by pilgrims making their way up Mount Zion to the Temple for worship. Going through these psalms helped to prepare worshippers for the richness of their time in God's presence. These psalms reminded each worshipping pilgrim of the character of God. As they sang them, they recited God's great acts of salvation in the past, and looked forward to the fulfillment of the prophetic promises in the ages to come. These joyful songs are like the first movement in a symphony. They open the way into the full experience of a great masterpiece. As these psalms were sung, people got caught up in the great symphony of God's praise. As they physically moved higher and higher toward the Temple on Mount Zion, they were being lifted higher and higher spiritually. It is like that with our great songs of praise and worship. These songs are woven together into a great symphony of praise and worship, giving us an opportunity to get into the correct spirit and frame of mind for spending time with our Father, God.

THE FIRST MOVEMENT

Taking your cue from the psalms, begin with words which remind you of the character of God. First, think about who God is—His glory and His goodness. Next, think about the awesome privilege of serving this God of grace, mercy and love. Then, think about Him and His patience, longsuffering and grace which He has shown us throughout our lifetimes. Finally, reflect on His justice and righteousness, which are always tempered with love and grace. So, first of all, you reflect on the inspiring character of God. Singing the praise songs which highlight God's character should be at the beginning of your journey to the Secret Place.

When you have ascended to a certain level acknowledging who God is (His awesome character), then you begin to sing the songs of God's historical work with you—what He has done for you in the past. You may want to reflect on His awesome work in the creation of the world and all that is contained in it. You may spend time remembering how He maintains and sustains the creation and all forms of life. I enjoy looking at the pictures sent back from the Hubble telescope, and the pictures of the universe available on the NASA website. As I look at them, I am in awe of the magnitude of the galaxies and the billions of stars which are millions of miles apart. Some are so far from Earth that the light you are looking at tonight departed from that star over 4,000 years ago. After many light years, your view of that star is just now arriving where you are located. When you reflect on the magnitude of that, and look at the nebulae and the amazing variety of the galaxies, you realize that God's work is so very awesome. When I acknowledge that God created all of that, I just want to praise Him for the majesty of what He has done.

I want to praise Him because He not only created our world, but He also provides for it. The psalms remind us that He even feeds the wild animals we may never see. These animals have no need for our help, because our gracious God feeds them and cares for them. Without His provision they would die of starvation. Without Him providing air for them, they would suffocate. Without His provision of water, they would die of dehydration.

When we reflect on His provision for us, we are filled with gratitude, and we are inspired to praise Him for His daily provision.

As we continue the ascent up the Mount Zion of our hearts, we remember and recite His great plan of salvation which was established before the foundation of the Earth. This plan has been His work from beginning to end. Through no work of our own hands, we have received salvation by grace alone. It has all been God's magnificent work through Christ alone. When you do this, you acknowledge that He has a plan for your life.

> *"'For I know the plans I have for you,' declares the LORD, 'plans to prosper you and not to harm you, plans to give you hope and a future. Then you will call upon me and come and pray to me, and I will listen to you. You will seek me and find me when you seek me with all your heart.'"* (Jeremiah 29:11-13, NIV)

The plan has not changed over time and it will never be altered. It is a plan to help you and not to harm you. It is a plan which gives you hope and a future. As we become more and more aware, we begin to praise Him for being a trustworthy God. Over and over, He has demonstrated that we can trust Him. We know from experience that there is no promise proceeding from the mouth of the Father that will ever fail. He is trustworthy and true in all His Word, and we know that He will be with us in all of our future and in all eternity.

We also know that this plan gives us access to the Father. That access is granted to all who call upon Him and seek Him wholeheartedly.

After reflecting on all God has done, you are prepared to affirm what your faith tells you He will do for you—as well as all His creation—in the future. As you profess your faith in God's care for your future, you are inspired to give thanks with more intensity. You confess your trust in Him and for Him. You confess His favor and blessing in your life. Each confession builds your faith and gives great power and clarity to the next affirmation. A great source for appropriate words to use in your praise is the Bible. An in-depth knowledge of the Bible is the key to this process. The more you know about God's Word, the more you have faith for the future. The more you see of what He has done for others, the more clearly you see what He plans to do for you. At last you realize that He plans to give you more than all you can ask or imagine.

> *"Now to him who is able to do immeasurably more than all we ask or imagine, according to his power that is at work within us, to him be glory in the church and in Christ Jesus through-out all generations, for ever and ever! Amen."* (Ephesians 3:20-21, NIV)

That is the first movement in the symphony. To keep moving toward the Secret Place, we need to continue to sing the songs of ascent as we move up the mountain of God.

THE SECOND MOVEMENT

The next movement in the symphony is to enter through the gates of His temple. At this point you need to know the password. Contrary to some popular thought, the password is not, "Gimme, Gimme!" Psalm 100:4a, (NIV), gives the password. It is, *"Enter his gates with thanksgiving."* Thanksgiving is the only way you can get through the gates and into His courts. Many people struggle here. Gratitude is not easy for many people. They have never been taught gratitude, nor have they learned it on their own initiative.

Some believe they are self-made. They honestly think that everything they own or have achieved came by their own talent, hard work, ingenuity, and cleverness. They ask, "Why should I thank someone else for what I have done?" As a result of these attitudes, they just can't experience feelings of gratitude. Their "self-made man or woman" approach fails to account for the origin of their talents and abilities. What they fail to understand is that just a slight change in the chemical content of one brain synapse can bring all that brilliance, cleverness, and ingenuity down. They need to understand that all of their abilities are gifts from God, and it is God who sustains them.

> *"But remember the Lord your God, for it is he who gives you the ability to produce wealth, and so confirms his covenant, which he swore to your forefathers, as it is today."* (Deuteronomy 8:18, NIV)

Until people come to the realization that God is the source of their strength and ability, they will be unable to fully experience gratitude and truthfully give the thanks our Lord so richly deserves. David clearly acknowledged that his success was a gift from God in Psalm 18:34 (also 2 Samuel 22:35), *"He teaches my hands to make war, so that my arms can bend a bow of bronze."* David knew that his ability, skill, and strength came from God. Goliath's sword was too large and heavy for David after he took it from the giant. Later, after God had trained and strengthen him, he retrieved the sword and used it skillfully and effectively. If you want to experience intimacy with God in the Secret Place, gratitude is the key which gets you through the door. Recognizing, thanking and praising the Lord as the source of every positive outcome in your life and ministry is the key to becoming that grateful person who is welcome in the Secret Place. Without genuine thanksgiving, you cannot make it through the gates into the courtyard.

Some people cannot experience gratitude because they don't believe they have been given their "fair share" in life. They hold to the belief that life has somehow shortchanged them. They don't believe they got the big breaks like others they know. Many people with this attitude have been sitting around waiting for a break for many years. It never seems to occur to them that others have worked hard and pressed for a long time to get an opportunity to succeed. Resentment builds out of this mindset. Resentment will block the heart from becoming grateful. For people with this attitude, it is almost impossible to well up any sense of gratitude because they truly believe that they have been let down by life, by God, and everyone else. They believe in their hearts that this is someone else's fault, and they fail to see that they are the ones who need to make a change. Since they believe that someone else is at fault, they are unlikely to seek or accept suggestions for change in their attitudes. Tragically, they cannot open the gates to the Secret Place until this issue is resolved, because they will not be allowed through the gates without heartfelt gratitude. It will never happen. We all need to learn this very important truth.

Spiritual pilgrims seeking entrance into the Secret Place of the Most High need to learn another important truth.

> *"Be still, and know that I am God; I will be exalted among the nations, I will be exalted in the earth!"* (Psalm 46:10)

This is a serious challenge for some people. They don't intend to be still, because they are active and action oriented. People have told me that God will just have to accommodate their way, because they don't intend to accommodate His. However, I want you to know this is not an option. One day, everyone will be confronted with this truth. One day, every knee will bow and every tongue will confess that Jesus Christ

41

is Lord. It is far better to learn it now, develop an attitude of gratitude, open the gates of God's Secret Place and experience the joy of His presence now, before it is too late.

THE THIRD MOVEMENT

The third movement in the symphony for gaining access to the Secret Place is to enter His courts with praise. Again, we look to Psalm 100 for the password that will take us to the next level. The psalmist tells us that after we pass through the gates, the next step is to enter the courtyard. We do this by a process of praise.

> *"and his courts with praise; give thanks to him and praise his name."* (Psalm 100:4b, NIV)

Notice that in this movement you do not stop giving thanks. You will move to a deeper level of intimacy by adding praise to your thanksgiving. At this level, words of gratitude have been forged into deep expressions of praise. In reality, we praise most what we are most grateful for receiving.

> *"And Jesus answered and said to him, 'Simon, I have something to say to you.' So he said, 'Teacher, say it.' 'There was a certain creditor who had two debtors. One owed five hundred denarii, and the other fifty. And when they had nothing with which to repay, he freely forgave them both. Tell Me, therefore, which of them will love him more?' Simon answered and said, 'I suppose the one whom he forgave more.' And He said to him, 'You have rightly judged.'"* (Luke 7:40-43)

The more clarity we have about our gratitude, the more we are enabled to feel and express the praise God so richly deserves.

Here, in the courtyard, there is the temptation to feel a sense of completion. Many songs and testimonies lead us to believe that when we get to the courtyard we have arrived at our final destination. After all, getting into God's courtyard is a giant step and it's easy to believe the task is done. But as you spend time in the courts, you begin to notice that there is a lot more going on just ahead. Some people are going beyond where you have stopped. Some people seem to be enjoying a much greater sense of joy in their intimacy with God. You notice the wall in front of you, and that beyond the wall there is smoke and a smell like someone is having a barbeque. The sights, sounds, and smells begin to build a hunger to go further. As you press in for more, you begin to step into the fourth and final movement of the symphony.

THE FINAL MOVEMENT

The final movement takes you into the most holy place (Secret Place). There is only one way to get there, but what is it? This step is only made through the pure worship of God. The key to this was given earlier in Psalm 100.

> *"Worship the Lord with gladness; come before him with joyful songs."* (Psalm 100:2, NIV)

Worship gets you inside the Secret Place. When you are finally able to experience this deep level of worship, you find your way into His presence. Then you realize that this is the only way you can truly come into an intimate relationship with Him. Too many people attempt to begin here. They try to jump to this place before their hearts are fully prepared. It is the discipline learned and practiced in the first three movements which prepares you to be in His presence.

Many people lack the patience to go through all the movements. They just want to jump in, get it done, and move on. I know people who would like to parachute or repel into God's presence. To them, it is just quicker and more efficient. We are accustomed to quick service and instant results. And after we go through these steps once, we build an expectation that next time we can bypass some of the steps to get there quicker. But it just doesn't work any other way. You can't jump to that place because your heart is not ready. If you try to jump into that place without your heart being ready, everything may just stop. You must develop the discipline of the first three parts, those first three movements, to get to the heart of this masterpiece.

WEARING THE PROPER ATTIRE

Now, to come into the secret place you have to be attired correctly. For people today, the attire is rather strange looking. We come into the Secret Place covered in blood; that is, covered with the blood of Jesus. In ancient times, they rehearsed this in the old temple. When the priests were allowed to enter the most holy place, everything had to be done exactly according to God's specified procedures. Only once each year could one priest enter the Most Holy Place, and that was done by lot.

The priest who went into the presence had to have special attire. Bells were sewn into the hem of the garment so his movement could be detected. The room had to be filled with incense so he could only see what he was allowed by God to see. If he did anything unholy, he knew that he would die. They kept the one selected by lot in the Temple for seven days to ensure that he was clean. The night before entering, he was kept awake all night to prevent even an unclean dream from disqualifying him. In addition to all of this, he had to have blood in his hands and on his garments.

You don't just charge into God's presence. You don't just casually rush into His Secret Place. You have to go in according to proper etiquette. You have to have a blood covering and wear priestly robes. But how do you get these priestly garments and the blood covering?

Do you realize that Jesus Christ was anointed to provide these garments for you? In fact, Jesus has provided for all of these procedural demands in order to give you access to the presence of God.

> *"But if we walk in the light as He is in the light, we have fellowship with one another, and the <u>blood of Jesus Christ His Son cleanses us</u> from all sin."* (1 John 1:7)

> *"Therefore, brothers, since we have confidence to enter the Most Holy Place by the blood of Jesus, by a new and living way opened for us through the curtain, that is, his body, and since we have a great priest over the house of God, let us draw near to God with a sincere heart in full assurance of faith, <u>having our hearts sprinkled to cleanse us</u> from a guilty conscience and having our <u>bodies washed with pure water</u>. Let us hold unswervingly to the hope we profess, for he who promised is faithful."* (Hebrews 10:19-23, NIV)

In the Secret Place, we are wearing our priestly robes. Jesus was anointed to provide a garment of praise for those who seek to enter the presence of the Lord. He read this passage from Isaiah 61 and declared that it was a reference to His work.

> *"The Spirit of the Lord GOD is upon Me, Because the Lord has anointed Me To preach good tidings to the poor; He has sent Me to heal the broken-hearted, To proclaim liberty to the captives, And the opening of the prison to those who are bound; To proclaim the acceptable year of the Lord, And*

*the day of vengeance of our God; To comfort all who mourn, To console those who mourn in Zion, To give them beauty for ashes, The oil of joy for mourning, The **garment of praise** for the spirit of heaviness; That they may be called trees of righteousness, The planting of the Lord, that He may be glorified."* (Isaiah 61:1-3)

We enter His presence with the righteousness provided by Jesus Christ.

"God made him who had no sin to be sin for us, so that in him <u>we might become the righteousness of God</u>." (2 Corinthians 5:21, NIV)

Most of us have a difficult time looking into a mirror and saying, "Oh, look! There is the righteousness of God." But that is exactly what Jesus has done for you. The key phrase here is "in him." Jesus provided the blood, the garments, and the righteousness so that you and I could go into the holy place—the Secret Place of the Most High. And this is how we get inside. Paul makes another strong point about how we are to see ourselves in a mirror. Remember it is not about us and what we have done. It is about Jesus and what He has done for us so that we are able to draw near to Father God.

"But we all, with unveiled face, beholding as in a mirror the glory of the Lord, are being transformed into the same image from glory to glory, just as by the Spirit of the Lord." (2 Corinthians 3:18)

Here, in a personal encounter, we learn a deeper truth. HERE in the Secret Place, we (Psalm 100:3a) *"know that the Lord is God."* We also learn that we are not God. Then we understand the cry of the people on Mount Carmel, *"The Lord,*

He is God." All doubt has been left behind. It has all been burnt in the fire of His glory. Here, we're in His presence. We are truly "home at last!" We have become what Jesus set out to accomplish for us. We have become the very righteousness of God through Him, and we are standing in the throne room with the Bridegroom.

We experience firsthand the "peace that passes all understanding." In the Secret Place of the most high there is no hurry or anxiety, and there are no appointments to rush away to meet. There are no time constraints and there are no late arrivals. There is no stress, no pressure, and no desire to be anywhere else. And now, with our full attention focused on Him, He can finally guide us into all truth.

For those who are willing to accept this invitation, I remind you to spend time quietly waiting for the Lord to respond. Many people pray fervently as they list all their needs and requests in minute detail. Then they move to prayers of intercession and name everyone they know who has a need. After this, they pray for people they don't know, but have heard about through friends or email messages. After exhausting themselves and their list, they say, "Amen!" and get up to go about their business.

When you are truly in the Secret Place, you are not even slightly tempted to pray like this. In the Secret Place, you know that it is totally unnecessary. In this Place, you know in the depth of your spirit that you know and are known by Almighty God. You don't have to go through a laundry list of every possible need with the God who knows everything about you, loves you totally, and is more than willing to meet all your needs. You realize that He already knows all these situations and has provided the power to support every faith request given in Jesus' name. Here, you know that you know that you know that you know all you need to know. The only driving desire is to be intimately connected with the Father. The only thing to do is worship Him for eternity and enjoy His presence forever. There are no questions that seem relevant or appropriate. Remember the words of Zephaniah:

> *"Be silent before the Sovereign LORD, for the day of the LORD is near. The LORD has prepared a sacrifice; he has consecrated those he has invited."* (Zephaniah 1:7, NIV)

Learning to be silent before the Sovereign Lord is very good advice. We need to be quiet, to be still, and to know that He is God. Remember the Lord has prepared the sacrifice and the Lord is the one who sends out the invitations. The Lord told me to write this book so that you would also know that you have been invited.

You need to learn and practice kingdom protocol. If you are going to meet with leadership from other nations as an ambassador, you have to learn the protocol of each nation. You do this in order to avoid awkward situations which would be embarrassing to the leaders of your own government. In the same way, you need to learn kingdom protocol before attempting to visit the King of Kings and Lord of Lords. Many Christians have lost "the fear of the Lord." They seem to believe that they don't have to fear Him anymore, because they have a special and unique loving relationship. Acting on this idea is totally unbiblical and very dangerous. Every promise of the Bible is conditional. Everything is conditional on obedience and a deep respect (fear) for the King of the Universe.

We live in an age that has lost the art of honoring fathers and mothers. We do not honor our leaders, our pastors, or anyone in the public eye. We seem to revel in scandals and malicious gossip. We like to see the powerful brought low and all their personal failures brought to light. We have lost respect and awe for those who have been created and loved by God. We have lost respect for those who are anointed by God and serve in anointed positions. Somewhere along the way, we have also lost that deep respect and awe for God. Many people believe it is okay to be totally casual with Him, and to talk with him as to a peer. However, the Word of God advises otherwise. It is wise to operate with Zephaniah's advice. In the awesome presence of our Holy God, be silent.

People tell me that they storm Heaven with their prayers. At first, that has a ring of authentic worship. However, on further reflection, storming someone's house doesn't seem very respectful. Would you appreciate someone who stormed your house? In Korea and in Asia, I visited several palaces. They all have a secret place, a secret garden, or a secret area of privacy for the royal family. In Korea, there is a beautiful old palace (KyongBok Palace) with a small, manmade island. It was constructed centuries ago, and it is surrounded by a moat. The water in the moat is covered with lilies which sometimes look like stepping stones to cross the small barrier of water. On the island is a beautiful little building and I always wanted to go out and look into this beautiful little house. Most Americans are built this way. We wonder why we can't cross the little bridge and see what we want to see when we want to see it. But, out of respect, you don't cross that bridge. In the days of the kings and queens of Korea, if you tried to cross that bridge, you would immediately be killed. You just don't storm a place that belongs to a king. It simply isn't done. So what makes us think we can treat Almighty God this way?

When you are a guest in a royal place in another country, you learn to wait on those who give you access and guide you into an audience with an important person.

In the same way, we need to develop some respect and learn kingdom protocol. There is a method God has given us for coming into His presence. He is the Holy God. He is the holy Creator God of the Universe, and we need to show the respect that is due Him. We need to go in with hearts prepared, covered with the blood of Jesus and wearing the garments of praise. There is a time and a place for intercessory prayer. There is a time to make all our requests known. However, the Secret Place of the most High is not the place and when you are in His awesome and holy presence, it is not the time. Bombarding Him with requests is totally unnecessary when you realize that He knows what you need and when you need it. In truth, He knows this better than you know it.

In prayer, it is advisable not to speak with a lack of faith. Repeating the same prayers over and over gives a strong message that we don't have faith that God will answer. Many believe He can, but faith says that He will. Know that He knows and then know by faith that He will provide. God will never guide you where he does not provide for you. Have faith!

The Lord spoke to me and said, "Don't wear yourself out during a time of refreshing."

> *"But those who wait on the Lord shall <u>renew their strength</u>; they shall mount up with wings like eagles, they shall run and not be weary, they shall walk and not faint."* (Isaiah 40:31)

There is no doubt in this passage of scripture. In the presence of the Lord be still, be silent, and be patient in waiting on the Lord. Wait and receive the renewing strength of the Lord. It is more awesome than anything you can ask, think or imagine. Trust Him, and allow him to take you to deeper places in Him. He knows when you are ready and is faithful to accomplish it.

> *"Deep calls unto deep at the noise of Your waterfalls; all Your waves and billows have gone over me."* (Psalm 42:7)

The psalmist gives a wonderful description of how it really feels to be in God's presence. You experience waves and billows of His life force and cleansing love. It is like the billowing waves of the ocean not only flowing over you, but through you as well. In that moment, you feel a deep calling in your being, placed there from the very depths of God's heart. It begins with a desire and quickly becomes a driving hunger to go deeper into the presence of God.

If you want to experience God in this way, follow the steps outlined in Psalm 100. Use your Biblical authority to enter the Secret Place.

> *"And God raised us with Christ and seated us with him in the heavenly realms in Christ Jesus."* (Ephesians 2:6, NIV)

All the verbs in this passage are in the past tense. This has already happened for those who are in Christ. This is not something you wait to experience after death. He didn't do all of this and leave us without access to Him. You can know with certainty that you have a seat with Christ in the heavenly realms. Go there and visit it once in a while! Many of the seats are empty because the occupants have never used their Biblical authority to visit the Third Heaven and occupy their assigned seats. Consider another powerful scriptural authority for visiting in Heaven:

> *"For through him (Jesus) we both have access to the Father by one Spirit."* (Ephesians 2:18, NIV)

Try to grasp the full impact of this promise in the very depth of your soul. You have access with Jesus Christ to the Father by the Holy Spirit who has been given to you. It is God's Word. Stand on it! Place a claim on this promise, and wait for the Lord to call you up into His presence! Amen!

My most sincere advice is: Don't wait any longer to wait on the Lord! Meet Him in the Secret Place and spend time with Him now. The time is NOW. Be in His presence now. Seek His face now. Get into the Secret Place now. Time spent with Him is eternal time. Time not spent with Him is just past time. Don't waste any more eternal time. Find your way to the Secret Place. Use the steps which God has generously provided. Out of a deep heart desire, begin to plan times to be with Him. Do whatever it takes to spend eternal time with Him, now. Follow the principles in Psalm 100 to get there with your heart ready to meet Him. Here is one more passage giving us Biblical authority to visit in Heaven. Place a claim on this passage too. Sometimes, I quote all three of these passages as I ask the Holy Spirit to give me access.

> *"Seeing then that we have a great High Priest who has passed through the heavens, Jesus the Son of God, let us hold fast our confession. For we do not have a High Priest who cannot sympathize with our weaknesses, but was in all points tempted as we are, yet without sin. Let us therefore come boldly to the throne of grace, that we may obtain mercy and find grace to help in time of need."* (Hebrews 4:14-16)

As you study this passage from the book of Hebrews, you need to answer one important question. Where is the "throne of grace" located? It is in Heaven, and the only way you can go before it is to visit in the Third Heaven.

When our military command went into wartime positioning, we started to have meetings at 5:00 a.m. In order to be there and ready with my answers to the task given the previous night, I had to leave my house at 4:00 a.m. In a situation like this, do I have time to spend time with God in the morning? The answer is absolutely, "Yes!" One of my disciplines has been that no matter what time it has to be, no matter what stress comes during the day, no matter how little sleep I get, I am going to spend time with God. So whatever time I was required to be present for duty, I backed up two hours and rose from sleep in order to spend time with God. We have to find a way. We have to be disciplined. You can't be a disciple without being disciplined. To discipline yourself, don't wait to wait on the Lord. Don't waste time. Don't let go of precious eternal time. Spend it with Him.

You have an invitation and God is crying out through so many sources and through so many people, "I want to spend time with you! Will you come and spend time with me? Can you carve out some time for me?" This is God's invitation. What is your response? What will you choose?

If you make the choice to discipline yourself to be in His presence, don't ignore the proper steps to get into the Secret Place. Remember, we are told to enter His gates with thanksgiving and His courts with praise and thanksgiving. We need to move from the natural world into the spiritual realm of God with thanksgiving. This puts us in the proper mood and perspective to meet with Him in holy intimacy. As we shift into deep praise, we move into His holy place where we truly make a spiritual connection with Him. I believe that we need to take a couple of additional steps. We need to worship Him so deeply that it opens the ancient door into the Secret Place, and then moves us into the Most Holy Place.

PRAYER

Father God, what an awesome privilege; what an honor to be invited to your throne room! I've been blocked out of some throne rooms. I wasn't on the invitation list in this lowly, little, earthly kingdom. But you Lord, have opened up Heaven for each and every one of us. Father God, please call to each of our hearts and help us, Lord, to find a way to your Secret Place. Lift us up into your throne room! Father God, we have open minds and open hearts. Teach us the principles of the kingdom. Teach us kingdom protocol. Teach us how to carry your kingdom in this world. Father God, we pray this in the awesome name of *Yeshua ha Messiach*, because we want your kingdom to come on Earth as it is in Heaven. Hear our prayer! Amen and Amen!

CHAPTER THREE

A VICTORY IN VIEW

"And I saw something like a sea of glass mingled with fire, and those who have the victory over the beast, over his image and over his mark and over the number of his name, standing on the sea of glass, having harps of God. They sing the song of Moses, the servant of God, and the song of the Lamb, saying: 'Great and marvelous are Your works, Lord God Almighty! Just and true are Your ways, O King of the saints! Who shall not fear You, O Lord, and glorify Your name? For You alone are holy. For all nations shall come and worship before You, For Your judgments have been manifested.'" (Revelation 15:2-4)

MONDAY MORNING (September 14), I RECEIVED AN ADDITIONAL VISION.

As I continued to seek wisdom and revelation concerning the kingdom lessons God has for us, I received another vision from the Lord. In this vision, I found myself in a futuristic-looking war room.

When we think about spiritual warfare, we tend to frame our thoughts around how Roman soldiers dressed and fought during the time of Jesus and the Apostles. The truth is that we have much more effective weapons of war and more efficient strategies for warfare today than at any time in the Roman Empire. I believe that God's plan for warfare is even more futuristic than we have experienced to date. The setting for this vision concerning spiritual warfare was clearly expressive of that reality.

In this vision, I was in a room similar to something you might see in a science fiction movie depicting a starship "Command Center." This room was an incredibly advanced war room with technology far beyond what is available today. In science fiction movies, the rooms are often poorly lit to prevent you from seeing how cheaply the set was made. The intensity of the light in this room was much greater than on any movie set. The room was brightly lit, and I was able to see every part of it down to the smallest detail. This was another Ultra HD vision, and all of the walls and furnishings were very clearly visible and were ultra-bright.

In this room, 13 people (including me) had gathered around a large, elliptically-shaped table. On the top of the table was a 3-D map of a future battleground with moveable pieces depicting friendly and enemy forces, weapons, equipment, and facilities. The group around the table seemed to be deeply involved in making plans for a battle which would soon take place in the region depicted on the map. Everyone was gazing intently at a scenario laid out on the table for the coming battle.

Suddenly, the person at the center of the table on the opposite side from where I was standing straightened up. He had a fixed stare on his face and seemed to be looking to a distant place beyond this room. He took a small step back. He raised His right hand slightly above His head, made a fist, and brought His arm and hand down quickly as He proclaimed joyously, "Yes! They're finally getting it!"

At this point, I realized that this person was the commander in chief, none other than Jesus Christ himself. After making that first comment, He stepped back again and then quickly moved to the side of the table on my right. He turned away from the group and faced the wall, which was actually a very large, brightly lit, interactive 3-D map of the entire universe. You could see all of the galaxies. It was as if this entire picture was alive on the wall. As King Jesus stood in front of this interactive depiction of the whole universe, He continued to speak.

King Jesus said, "They have been satisfied with the outcome of a few small battles and little skirmishes, most of which they initiated on their own. Many of these had little or nothing to do with my strategy or my published plan. As yet, they haven't seen the big picture and they haven't submitted fully to my leadership. But, now! Now, they're finally seeing the truth. They're beginning to line up with my plan. Now, they're ready to watch my final victory. And, they won't even have to fight. But, like the army of Jehoshaphat, they just need to suit up and show up. Then they can watch as I defeat all the enemy forces."

Are you ready for this kind of spiritual battle? The key that released the power of God to bring this awesome victory for Jehoshaphat and Judah was worship. The praise team led the army. Their song was based on the prayers of the people at the dedication of the Temple, which brought down the glory presence of the Lord in a cloud. Praise is an awesome weapon of spiritual war. You can give thanks and praise followed by worship in the Third Heaven and release powerful forces for victory on Earth. Isn't that awesome? I know some intercessors that are doing Second Heaven intercession and experiencing all kinds of injuries as they battle principalities and powers over which they have no authority. I'm ready for more Third Heaven intercession, which releases the awesome power of the Seven Spirits of God and the legions of angels in the heavenly host. How about you?

As I contemplated the vision of the heavenly war room, I thought, *You know, victorious living is so rare today.* Maybe you have noticed this too. Perhaps like me you have wondered, where is the victory we are supposed to be experiencing? In many churches, I hear a great deal of talk about the power of the enemy. I get offended by this kind of talk. Next to my Jesus, the devil is nothing. I hear people complain about how the enemy's attacks are keeping them from the blessings God has for them. I hear them talking about how the enemy's attacks are robbing them of their health, or how these attacks are hurting their loved ones. When you are standing in the Third Heaven with Jesus, this seems like incredibly foolish talk. We need to realize that the victory has already been won. We have a defeated enemy. That's the kind of enemy I like. He can only operate by deception. He can only operate if he can steal some authority from you, because God has given back all the authority to Jesus. And Jesus said:

> *"Behold, I give you the authority to trample on serpents and scorpions, and over all the power of the enemy, and nothing shall by any means hurt you."* (Luke 10:19)

I like to pay close attention to what Jesus is saying. I will take His word over the words of all others. As I listen to many sick, tired, and whipped intercessors, I get the feeling they have more respect for the power of the devil than the power of Jesus. They trust what some man said about the power of the enemy and forget what Jesus said. They forget what Paul said:

> *"The God of peace will soon crush Satan under your feet. The grace of our Lord Jesus be with you."* (Romans 16:20, NIV)

We are from the seed of Eve and our destiny is to crush Satan under our feet. We are the disciples of *Yeshua ha Messiach*, who came to destroy the works of the devil, and it is our task to carry on His work. Amen? When we confess the power of the enemy, we're giving our authority back to him. Then he has legal authority to harass and oppress us. I don't plan to do that. I don't confess any power for him or any authority for him. I confess that I have authority over ALL of the power of the enemy. I believe Jesus! How about you?

I like to ask people if they really believe these things the Bible teaches about the believer's authority over the works of the devil. Most quickly say, "Yes!" But, what exactly do they believe? Do they just believe that Jesus said it or do they believe that it is really true? So many people do not live or act on Jesus' statements about our authority over the enemy. Do they really believe His words are true? I regularly hear Christian people speaking from a victim mentality. They speak of their helplessness against spiritual forces. This is such foolish talk. If you are unable to handle a little demon (scorpion), then what are you going to do when you meet Satan, himself? We must begin to believe the Word of God. If we believe that these words of Jesus are true—if we believe that we have authority over all the forces of the enemy—it's time to start living like we believe it, start talking like we believe it, and start praying like we believe it.

In the Third Heaven, all this talk of Satan's power is so foolish. During an extended praise and worship service, I found myself lifted in the spirit to the Third Heaven. It was awesome! I saw the 10,000 times 10,000 and thousands of thousands of angels worshipping God. It was beyond anything I had ever imagined. All of Heaven was responding to the worship coming up from Earth and adding gloriously to that praise. In the distance, I heard a voice crying out. It was coming from the worship service where my body was still located. The worship leader was talking about dealing with the devil. Everyone in Heaven looked at each other with a puzzled look and exclaimed, "Who?" In the Third Heaven, Satan is not even a distant memory. He is lost from there. He will never return to that place. He just doesn't matter there. And we need to develop that mentality. Refuse to acknowledge him and absolutely refuse to give any of your authority (purchased at a great price by our Lord, Jesus) back to that undeserving serpent, the devil.

> *"And He said to them, 'I saw Satan fall like lightning from heaven. Behold, I give you the authority to trample on serpents and scorpions, and over all the power of the enemy, and nothing shall by any means hurt you.'"* (Luke 10:18-19)

So there are some things I would like for you to remember.

THE VICTORY HAS BEEN WON

The first thing I want you to remember is that the victory has already been won! Amen! Our victory was won almost 2,000 years ago on the cross. It was a sovereign act of a just and holy God so that He could deal with sinful people, reconcile them to Himself and be able to dwell with them again. We need to grasp this beautiful truth—He wants us to be with Him. He wants us to be in fellowship with Him. He wants us to come to the Third Heaven and spend time with Him. In order to make this happen, He has taken care of the sin problem once and for all. Jesus died to remove our sin and make this possible. His death paid the penalty for all our iniquity. He paid for every bit of it—not just part of it! His death set us free from the bondage to fear and death. His death gave us victory over the enemy forever and ever. Amen!

When Jesus died on that cross, several critical things became realities in our lives. By the stripes given to Him, we were healed. By the bruises that He took, our iniquities were taken care of forever. By the beating He took, our peace was established. The victory has been won. We need to quit acting as if we are still fighting a battle which He has already won.

Don't let the death of Jesus be in vain! Don't be tricked into taking up your shame and guilt again. By our actions and talk, we make it seem like we go up to the cross, see our shame and guilt nailed to that old cross, and then reach up and take them back. It is as if we say, "Jesus, thank you for holding these for a little while. I needed that breather, but now I'll just take them back and continue to be weighed down by them." Don't do that! Don't let shame or guilt from the past rob you of your victory in Jesus. Don't allow yourself to be led back into bondage to fear. Stand on the victory! Stand on the promises of Jesus!

Whatever you do, don't snatch defeat out of the jaws of victory. Do you watch and like the commercials during the Super Bowl? So much money is invested to craft those in just the right way to catch our attention, but they don't always work as expected. One of those commercials from the past was a Mountain Dew commercial. Maybe you remember it. A man chased a cheetah across the plain to get his canned soft drink back. After he ran the big cat down, he reached into that cheetah's mouth and pulled the can out. After the Super Bowl, people were asked about which commercials they liked best, and almost everyone mentioned this commercial. It was really catchy, but it was a complete failure. It was a failure because almost every single person remembered seeing a can of Pepsi rather than Mountain Dew being drawn out of the cheetah's mouth. It got their attention, but it literally snatched defeat out of the jaws of victory. Sometimes I wonder, just what we are snatching out of the mouth of the enemy?

> "*I have told you these things, so that in me you may have peace. In this world you will have trouble. But take heart! I have overcome the world.*"
> (John 16:33, NIV)

Many people only quote: "*In this world you will have trouble.*" They leave off the intention stated at the beginning and the critically important conclusion. Jesus is trying to focus on the peace that He brings, but so many people disagree. They claim that this scripture is about all the trouble you are going to have in this world. They begin to moan about how you are going to be hurt in the world and focus on all the harm that is coming to you in this life. They point to all the attacks coming from the enemy and all the pain and suffering coming to you, your family, your church, and all your friends. This is not even close to what Jesus was trying to say. Jesus makes it plain that He is saying this so that we might have peace. So take heart. He has overcome the world. The victory has already been won. Jesus has overcome the world. Instead of doubt, we need to give Him praise! Thank you, Jesus, for winning the battle! Thank you for the victory! We need to learn to be victorious Christians. I have the victory! How about you? Not only has the victory been won, but it has been announced for such a long time. Listen to the words of 1 Chronicles 29:11!

> *"Yours, O Lord, is the greatness, the power and the glory, the victory and the majesty; for all that is in heaven and in earth is Yours; Yours is the kingdom, O Lord, and You are exalted as head over all."*

So remember that the victory has already been won!

WHO WON THE VICTORY?

The second thing I want you to remember is who won the victory. When we remember this and reflect on this truth, it builds our faith. We need to constantly focus on building our faith and maintaining it always.

> *"Oh, sing to the Lord a new song! For He has done marvelous things; His right hand and His holy arm have gained Him the victory."* (Psalm 98:1)

As we focus on ourselves, victory can seem fleeting. This happens when we listen to the enemy point out our weaknesses and mistakes from the past. If we're not careful, we will start to agree with the enemy. When you agree with the enemy, you get the enemy's results, and you certainly don't want what he has to offer to you. So don't get into agreement with the enemy. Don't speak about defeat! Don't speak about your past failures! Don't bring up guilt and shame! If you want to talk about the past, bring up the enemy's past. Bring up how he used to be one of the choir leaders in Heaven—how he used to be one of the "morning stars." And look where he is now. Look at what a mess he made out of things. He lost that lofty position. So talk about his past, his present, and his future.

Only talk about your future in Christ. Keep your eyes fixed on Jesus! Hear His words! We know that He has the power! We know that He has the glory! We know that He has the authority! We know that He has the position, and we know that He is "the way, the truth, and the life." So speak the words of Jesus and not the words of the enemy.

Meditate on who Jesus is and come into agreement with Him. Agree with who He says He is. Then take on the really difficult part—Agree with who He says you are in Him. Live with an attitude of victory, and live with an attitude of gratitude.

In this position of gratitude, all fear is cast out. If you are truly grateful for the victory, how can you be afraid of the enemy who has already been defeated? Memorize and meditate on the following passage:

> *"But thanks be to God, who gives us the victory through our Lord Jesus Christ."* (1 Corinthians 15:57)

Do we have the victory? Absolutely! We should be grateful and constantly giving thanks to our God and the Father of our Lord Jesus Christ. As we give Him thanks for the victory, it anchors it in our hearts and our minds. It also releases its power through the law of confession.

Do not confess the words of a defeated enemy! This confession will not do anything positive for you or for anyone else. Instead, confess what the Word of God says.

So first of all, remember that we already have the victory. Then, secondly, remember who won the victory.

CLAIM THE VICTORY

The third thing I would like for you to do is to claim this victory in your life and in your ministry! Claim the victory and stand on it. Because when we're united with Christ, we are united in His death as well. Listen to what Paul says to the disciples at Corinth.

> *"For the love of Christ compels us, because we judge thus: that if One died for all, then all died; and He died for all, that those who live should live no longer for themselves, but for Him who died for them and rose again."* (2 Corinthians 5:14-15)

Did you catch that—they "all died." We have all died with him! We have all risen with Christ! And we have been seated with Him in heavenly places. If you are seated with Christ in Heaven, how can the devil hurt you? He can't get to you. He has been kicked out of Heaven and lost his access. So it's impossible for him to get to you and do any real harm! Do you believe this? You see, that is the real question. It is a matter of faith.

The Holy Spirit gives us a power gift to maintain this victory. If you have been born again of God, this promise is for you.

"For whatever is born of God overcomes the world. And this is the victory that has overcome the world—our faith." (1 John 5:4)

If we use it as God intended, FAITH is a powerful gift. It is a gift provided through the Holy Spirit. By faith, you overcome the world! By faith, you overcome the enemy. By faith, you overcome everything that comes against you. All you need in order to hold on to victory is to accept the gift. You don't have to work for it. You don't have to earn it. In fact, you can't work for it or earn it. It's a gift. Receive it from God, and through faith hold on to the victory.

We are all called of God to be overcomers. He has not made a mystery out of the method of overcoming. It has always been open. We read about it in 1 Chronicles. We read about it all through the Bible. He has not made it a mystery. He has, in fact, taught us the method for overcoming.

"And they overcame him by the blood of the Lamb and by the word of their testimony, and they did not love their lives to the death." (Revelation 12:11)

It is first and foremost through the blood of the Lamb, but you must add something to it. You have to add your own testimony. So, confess what the Word says. Confess it as your own victory. It is not enough for it to be someone else's victory. It has to be your victory. You must claim and hold on to that victory for yourself.

What is your testimony? I hear many people talking more about the enemy than about Jesus. If you listen to them for very long, you begin to think they are following the enemy. They talk about his awesome power. They talk about all his abilities. But he really doesn't have many abilities, and he hasn't really learned anything new. He still uses the same tricks he used in the Garden of Eden. He hasn't gotten any smarter. He's a dead spirit. He is not a living, creative spirit like God. His tricks are so predictable that you can read about them in the Bible, which was written centuries ago. There is no excuse for being tricked or surprised by him. God has revealed all of it to you. So what you need to do is testify that you are a victorious overcomer. Through Jesus Christ, you have the victory.

Are you fighting battles that have already been won? Don't do that! Your mission is to be a courageous kingdom carrier. Courageous kingdom carriers spread the victory! They are letting others know that we don't have to be fighting these battles over and over. The victory has already been won. The battle is over. So help others receive the victory in their lives! Remember what Paul said:

> *"Yet in all these things we are more than conquerors through Him who loved us."* (Romans 8:37)

We all know this verse, but I wonder how many of us know what it really means. What does it mean to be *"more than conquerors"*? What do you do after you win the battle? After conquering, it is time to do nation building. This is what the children of Israel did after entering the Promised Land. They conquered and then built the nation. We have seen this more clearly in recent times. After winning the military battle in Iraq, the USA began to do nation building. Some thought this would be simple and easy. However, nation building is more difficult and challenging than winning the war. During this phase, you remain very vulnerable to resistance and sabotage from rebellious members of the former powers.

This is what we are doing now. We're building the kingdom of God in what used to be enemy territory.

> *"For all nations shall come and worship before You."* (Revelation 15:4)

Powerful military forces move quickly to defeat the large elements of the enemy's forces. Through shock and awe, they can bring down a small government or military force fairly quickly. If they stop to deal with every little group along the way, the mission will be seriously hindered. So they move quickly through the entire area in order to take out the large groups. But there will be remaining pockets of resistance. Many smaller, cleanup missions require small groups of soldiers to slowly, over time, reduce or halt resistance. During this phase, the remaining loyalist and enemy forces will send insurgents in to block the process.

This has been Satan's plan during all of human history. There is nothing mysterious here. We should expect to discover little pockets of resistance to our new lives and work in and for Christ. Don't be surprised if the enemy sends insurgents in to sabotage you. Little doubts are planted during this time. You will hear people say that nothing has changed. You didn't really win the battle. There really is no victory here. Then you find out that some people in your very own home camp will begin to lose heart and want to give up. They want to quit. They say that it costs too much, it's too bad, or it's too rough. This happens in our spiritual warfare with the enemy just like it happens in military campaigns.

So nation building is challenging. Don't give up! Go back to the heart of your faith. The victory has already been won. But we have gotten so focused on little skirmishes, the small battles. We begin to think that this is the whole war. The war is over. The victory has been won. Peace has been declared and we need to begin to live like that. Because to those who hold on until the end, there will be great victory. Remember Psalm 37:9, *"But, those who wait on the Lord, They shall inherit the earth."* In other words, all the nations will come to them. If you inherit the Earth, then all nations belong to you. It is no coincidence that we are called throughout scripture to take the nations for God. We are to build the kingdom of God in every nation so that God can have back His creation which mankind has given away.

Now for the really good news: The victory party has already been planned. Invitations have been sent out. Unfortunately, it is very much like the parable Jesus used of the great wedding feast. People are not responding to this great offer. They are too busy or have so many other things to do which seem more important at the moment.

Now, in the same way, God is inviting us (you and me) into the Secret Place (the Third Heaven) to receive from Him specific directions and a specific mission as part of the kingdom building on Earth. He wants to impart this training and these resources so we can accomplish our mission. If we work to accomplish this, His will is going to be done on Earth as it is in Heaven. Tragically, many remain who will not accept the invitation to a victory celebration.

If you are wondering what you can do, quit wondering. Go ask Jesus! Quit wondering! Let the Holy Spirit guide you into all truth. Because God is inviting you into His Secret Place to equip you as kingdom builders. He wants to refresh you and strengthen you as you wait on Him. He wants to heal you, renew you, resource you and teach you kingdom principles and kingdom strategies. And then He plans to send you out as ambassadors of the King of Kings. That is God's call to you in this present time.

> *"Now I saw heaven opened, and behold, a white horse. And He who sat on him was called Faithful and True, and in righteousness He judges and makes war. His eyes were like a flame of fire, and on His head were many crowns. He had a name written that no one knew except Himself. He was clothed with a robe dipped in blood, and His name is called The Word of God. And the armies in heaven, clothed in fine linen, white and*

clean, followed Him on white horse. Now out of His mouth goes a sharp sword, that with it He should strike the nations. And He Himself will rule them with a rod of iron. He Himself treads the winepress of the fierceness and wrath of Almighty God. And He has on His robe and on His thigh a name written: KING OF KINGS AND LORD OF LORDS." (Revelation 19:11-16)

"And I saw the beast, the kings of the earth, and their armies, gathered together to make war against Him who sat on the horse and against His army. Then the beast was captured, and with him the false prophet who worked signs in his presence, by which he deceived those who received the mark of the beast and those who worshiped his image. These two were cast alive into the lake of fire burning with brimstone. And the rest were killed with the sword which proceeded from the mouth of Him who sat on the horse." (Revelation 19:19-21)

Remember, you just have to suit up and show up, as in the days of Jehoshaphat. Even in the end-times scenario, at the end of the great tribulation, Jesus will win the battle. With one word coming out of His mouth, He will totally annihilate the millions of soldiers in the forces of the enemy. That's our Savior. That's our Lord. This is who we serve, and this is our victory. We need to stop fighting battles that have already been won and start claiming the victory. Stand with Jesus and believe. We need to get ourselves into a position to start going to the Third Heaven and become Third Heaven intercessors. We need to be those who have received—first hand—the counsel of God, and then be sent back to establish His kingdom on Earth. That's the mission we have! That's the victory which has already been won.

That is what He calls us to do. Are you ready for it?

PRAYER

"Finally, be strong in the Lord and in his mighty power. Put on the full armor of God so that you can take your stand against the devil's schemes. For my struggle is not against flesh and blood, but against the rulers, against the authorities, against the powers of this dark world and against the spiritual forces of evil in the heavenly realms. I therefore put on the full armor of God, so that when the day of evil comes, I may be able to stand my ground, and after I have done everything, to stand. I stand firm then, with the belt of truth buckled around my waist, with the breastplate of righteousness in place, and with my feet fitted with the readiness that comes from the gospel of peace. In addition to all this, I take up the shield of faith, with which I can extinguish all the flaming arrows of the evil one. I take the helmet of salvation and the sword of the Spirit, which is the word of God. And I pray in the Spirit on all occasions with all kinds of prayers and requests. With this in mind, I will be alert and always keep on praying ..." (Ephesians 6:10-18, NIV, paraphrased)

CHAPTER 4

CALLED TO BE VALIANT

W hile spending a few days in Jerusalem, our small group decided to go to the Western Wall each day to pray for Israel and for peace in Jerusalem. One very warm afternoon, we went from the hotel to the Jaffa Gate and walked through the old city to the Western Wall.

After praying for a time at the wall, I asked the Lord for a Divine encounter. This had happened before and I had every confidence it would happen again on that day. I placed the palms of my hands on the wall, leaned forward, and touched my forehead to the stone. As soon as my head made contact with the wall, it disappeared and I was in an underground tunnel. This vision was so realistic that I can only describe it as being translated to a different time and place by the power of the Holy Spirit.

I was standing in a large cavern, which was inside of a very long tunnel. The cavern had been well constructed by skilled workers. It had archways in all four directions leading away from this very ornately designed chamber. Three of the archways led into other, well-constructed and ornate sections of the tunnel. Somehow, I knew that I was supposed to go through the fourth archway which led to a slightly smaller and less ornate section. It was definitely the path which few people chose to travel.

Each successive section of the tunnel was smaller and less well-constructed. On the left there was a small staircase leading up to a small platform in front of a completely sealed door. On the other side of the platform, stairs went back down to the floor of the cave. I became very aware that the cave was going lower and lower. My thoughts went to a story I had been told about a man who spent several minutes in hell. I definitely didn't want to go into hell. The Spirit assured me that my journey was not into hell.

I continued and the cave got smaller and began to look more like a mineshaft. Ahead, I saw a pair of very old wooden doors. One was slightly open and a small amount of light was coming through the opening. I was now convinced that I was in the catacombs and would soon join a group of hidden worshippers in a time of great persecution. However, when I entered the door there was only one man there. He motioned for me to come over to him. I soon learned that it was Peter. He looked older than I had pictured him and it was obvious that he had endured much for his Lord.

I was excited about the possibilities of speaking with Peter and learning from his experiences. However, he did not say a word. He just handed me a sword. It was not pretty or ornamental. It was crude and obviously made hastily for one purpose — great spiritual warfare. I remembered something Peter wrote in his first letter, "You must be prepared and ready at all times. Don't let yourself be surprised!" (1 Peter 4:12-13, loosely paraphrased) This was the only wisdom available to me on this visit. Peter then pointed toward an upward pathway and gestured for me to go that way. This part of the cave was very different. It was steep and made of rows of square stones about 10 inches square. It looked like a Roman road. As I proceeded upward, the stones became more and more wet and slippery. The light ahead became red and I heard the horrible sounds of battle just beyond the opening. I then realized that it had been blood which had made the stones so slippery. Now blood was literally flying through the air, and I could hear the loud screams of pain as the wounded fell in battle. I knew that I was walking into an awful battle with blood, sweat, and great pain.

As I neared the opening into the battle, I saw a lone figure seated on the left side of the path. He was wearing a white robe and was glowing with the glory of God. It was my Lord and Savior, Jesus Christ. I was very much aware that He was not there to save me, but to prepare me for the battle. As I came up to Him, He extended His hand in blessing, I felt greatly empowered and blessed. At this point, I knew in my heart I was not going to survive this battle. I summoned all the strength and courage which Jesus had just imparted to me and stepped in the chaos, knowing that whatever happened I would be with Him forever.

As soon as I stepped through the opening, the vision shifted and I was in another room. It was not very large. It had a dome-shaped ceiling. The room had eight sides and there were stained glass windows on every wall. Each window had a box of beautiful flowers attached at the bottom part of the facing. The light coming through the windows gave the room a strange, purple-colored glow. It was really beautiful. I was very content until I tried to move and found that I was unable to do anything. The room was really nice. I felt an awesome peace in my soul. I had no pain. In fact, I couldn't feel anything at all. It was then that a stark realization hit me. I was lying down on a large stone, and I was dead. This room was some sort of tomb for those who had fallen in battle. I decided to make the best of it and enjoy the peace. After what seemed like a long period of time, a question came into my mind. How long was I going to be here? The only answer was: "I am dead and I am going to be here until Jesus returns!" I believe this would have been easier to handle if I was not fully conscious. I started to feel a little bit of panic, but then calmed myself with the assurance: "I am dead. Nothing bad can happen to me now!" The only task now was to figure out how to spend the time, since I had no idea how long this was going to last.

Suddenly a door opened behind my head. Something happened that was awesome. I was alive again. I stood up and tried out my legs and arms. Everything worked. Cool! Then I looked through the door and was almost frozen in awe at what I saw. I stepped through the door to get a better look. There in front of me was a column of white horses standing two abreast that went so far back in the distance that I could not see the end. The rider in the front stepped down off of His horse, and I knew who it was. I bowed before my Lord and Savior, Jesus Christ. Then He pointed to a horse without a rider and asked, "Are you ready to ride?" I was thrilled. I knew that I was going to ride back with the white robed army as Jesus returned for the Millennial reign. This was truly awesome. I stepped toward my horse and, suddenly, I was back at the Western Wall. I had forgotten that I had been there praying before this all unfolded.

Later, as I reflected on this experience, I knew that I had been given a great gift which I didn't recognize at first. I had literally gone through one of the most powerful sets of Biblical truths. I had lived it and now it was mine. I had died with Christ. I was buried with Christ, and I had been raised with Christ. I am now seated with Him in heavenly places. This is now my truth, and the enemy cannot take it away from me. I pray that you will come to know this truth as profoundly as I have. It changes everything when you know that you will live with Him forever. It is the absolute conviction which enables us to be valiant for the Lord. We have nothing to lose. We have everything to gain. Amen!

Most people like a good story or movie about someone who has done something considered heroic. We are especially charmed by an average, ordinary man or woman who rises to the occasion and bravely wins against overwhelming odds. Conversely, most people dislike the cowardly man or woman in the same story. There is something at least mildly repulsive about someone who has the opportunity to do something noble but allows fear to prevent them from making the best choice. Somehow these traits (liking heroes and disliking the cowards) seem to be built into the fabric of our human nature. Perhaps it is a part of being created in the image of God. According to the Bible, God doesn't care for cowards either.

> *"He said to me: 'It is done. I am the Alpha and the Omega, the Beginning and the End. To him who is thirsty I will give to drink without cost from the spring of the water of life. He who over-comes will inherit all this, and I will be his God and he will be my son. But the cowardly, the unbelieving, the vile, the murderers, the sexu-ally immoral, those who practice magic arts, the idolaters and all liars—their place will be in the fiery lake of burning sulfur. This is the second death.'"* (Revelation 21:6-8)

As you read verse eight from Revelation, Chapter 21, notice where the word *cowardly* is placed in this sentence. It is at the very top of the priority list of character flaws that will keep you from entering the heavenly kingdom. It is above the unbe-lieving, the vile, the murderers, the sexually immoral, and those who practice various forms of idolatry. Perhaps that seems a little harsh to you. This may be why our modern society has attempted to excuse and elevate cowardly behavior by labeling it in terms which are more sensitive, inclusive, and politically correct. We say they are not really cowardly. They are merely heroically challenged. But no matter how nicely we try to put it, cowards are still distasteful. They let others suffer, get hurt, or die because they will not take action.

Throughout the Bible, God has told his people not to fear or be dismayed. I found over 450 references in the Bible for the word *fear*. After reading through them, I found that most of these references were challenges to avoid being fearful. In like manner, there are many passages telling people to be strong and of good courage because God is with them. Battles will not be won by cowardly people. Testimonies will not be shared by those too afraid to speak out. Truth will not be upheld by those who fear the response of other people. They may know the truth. They may have an idea about what needs to be done. They may ask others to rescue them, but fear constantly prevents them from doing or saying the right thing at the crucial moment.

> *"No man shall be able to stand before you all the days of your life; as I was with Moses, so I will be with you. I will not leave you nor forsake you. Be strong and of good courage, for to this people you shall divide as an inheritance the land which I swore to their fathers to give them. Only be strong and very courageous, that you may observe to do according to all the law which Moses My servant commanded you; do not turn from it to the right hand or to the left, that you may prosper wherever you go."* (Joshua 1:5-7)

Fear is natural. People who are considered brave feel fear like everyone else, but they don't let it stop them from doing the right thing. Cowardly behavior, on the other hand, is a testimony to a lack of faith. Some do not trust God's promises of protection and provision. Some don't believe that God will be with them during the difficult times. Others are just immobilized by the fear of the unknown. People who truly trust God conquer fear. David proclaimed,

> *"The Lord is my light and my salvation; Whom shall I fear? The Lord is the strength of my life; of whom shall I be afraid?"* (Psalm 27:1)

As this chapter was being written, the Lord gave me a series of visions which came at such blinding speed that I cried out, "What was that? What just happened?" I knew that these visions had significant meaning, but they were just too fast. So I asked the Holy Spirit to show me again and tell me what they meant. I was immediately taken back to the first vision and then slowly moved through the next segment while the Holy Spirit guided my understanding.

The first vision was of a very high and rugged mountain peak. The scene was stark with no signs of life. Below me and all around the mountain peak were gathering clouds of deep darkness. It was as if some type of evil force was brooding over the face of the Earth. The clouds were threatening and violent in their movement. The Holy Spirit said, "Perilous times will come as the end time harvest is ushered in, and many people will cower in fear at the threatened violence of that hour."

"But know this, that in the last days perilous times will come: For men will be lovers of them-selves, lovers of money, boasters, proud, blas-phemers, disobedient to parents, unthankful, un-holy, unloving, unforgiving, slanderers, without self-control, brutal, despisers of good, traitors, headstrong, haughty, lovers of pleasure rather than lovers of God, having a form of godliness but denying its power. And from such people turn away! For of this sort are those who creep into households and make captives of gullible wom-en loaded down with sins, led away by various lusts, always learning and never able to come to the knowledge of the truth. Now as Jannes and Jambres resisted Moses, so do these also resist the truth: men of corrupt minds, disapproved concerning the faith; but they will progress no further, for their folly will be manifest to all, as theirs also was." (2 Timothy 3:1-9)

Through Paul, God has forewarned us of these times. Why

should we be surprised by them?

As this was still sinking into my mind, the Holy Spirit carried me with him at blinding speed to a small boat being tossed about by huge waves in a troubled sea. From the natural, this situation seemed hopeless. As if this was not a strong enough threat, the enemy threw a huge spear at the helpless people on the deck of the boat. The reason for the fast movement of the Holy Spirit had been for Him to arrive just in time to pull the people out of the path of the spear as it passed harmlessly by them. In my mind, I remembered these words from the book of Isaiah:

> *"When the enemy comes in,* [the position of the comma was changed to more accurately reflect the content of the message] *like a flood the Spirit of the Lord will lift up a standard against him."*
> (Isaiah 59:19b)

The Holy Spirit spoke to me saying, "This boat is a picture of the church. If the people of God look at the dark clouds, the storm, and the raging waves, they will be overcome by fear. But what is impossible for man is possible for God. I am your shield during these perilous times at the end of the age. You, too, are called to be a shield for the others. But, to do so, you must put on the whole armor of God every day."

> *"Stand therefore, having girded your waist with truth, having put on the breastplate of righteousness, and having shod your feet with the preparation of the gospel of peace; above all, taking the shield of faith with which you will be able to quench all the fiery darts of the wicked one. And take the helmet of salvation, and the sword of the Spirit, which is the word of God; praying always with all prayer and supplication in the Spirit, be-*

ing watchful to this end with all perseverance and supplication for all the saints…" (Ephesians 6:14-18a)

I didn't waste any time. I started suiting up to make myself ready for the mission I have been given in the service of our Lord in these last days. How can people possibly believe they will be able to stand alone without the Holy Spirit's help and without the armor He has given us? Every day, we must be vigilant to wear the armor and stand watch against the enemy's weapons. We are at war. The victory is certain! We must never forget that God has given us what we need to limit the damage, protect others, and survive the attacks of the enemy. Don't go to war unarmed and unprepared. God will be with you and the Holy Spirit will set up a standard against the enemy. And you are called to stand with the Holy Spirit alongside that same standard.

I pray that the Lord will give you the anointing of the sons of Issachar; to have wisdom to understand the times and to know what you and your church should do. I pray that the Lord will provide all you need to stand in these last days and give you the courage to remain standing until the end. Amen! Remember these words from Isaiah,

> *"If you do not stand firm in your faith, you will not stand at all."* (Isaiah 7:9b, NIV)

Like the US Marine Corps, the Lord is "looking for a few good men" and women who have the courage to stand against the enemy in these last days. The Lord is calling those who are willing to serve and to stand up as part of His valiant army. In these perilous times, it will take courage and faith to stand. Those who will be able to respond are the ones who trust the Lord and know that He will not leave them alone in the face of battle. They will have revelation knowledge to know and trust the Lord's promise:

*"…do not fear what they fear, and do not dread
it. The LORD Almighty is the one you are to re-
gard as holy, he is the one you are to fear, he is
the one you are to dread, and he will be a sanctu-
ary."* (Isaiah 8:12b-14a, NIV)

When Israel finally conquered the seven major enemy forces
and moved into the Promised Land, many expected that all the
battles were over. However, there was still much to do. God had
not allowed them to take the entire land because they were not
large enough to fill it and control it. So some of the enemy forces
remained in small pockets of resistance throughout the land.
Dealing with these forces was not easy and the war was never
fully won. Even some of the giants remained and had to be dealt
with in future battles. This is not uncommon. It even happens in
modern day warfare. The large forces move through and conquer the organized enemy forces, but some battles remain. Most
of these are small skirmishes as enemy strongholds are cleared
one by one. In some ways, this is more challenging than the big
war. Small groups can create much damage over time through
acts of terrorism. And during these times, we are called upon to
remain valiant to the finish. We have some encouragement from
the Bible:

*"Do not be afraid of them; the Lord your God him-
self will fight for you."* (Deuteronomy 3:22, NIV)

The qualifier is that He fights with you when it is His battle,
in accordance with His battle plan.

Many Christians have difficulty seeing God this way. They
think that the God of the New Testament is somehow different
from the God of the Old Testament. I would remind you of
Hebrews 13:8, "Jesus Christ *is* the same yesterday, today, and
forever." If you have seen Jesus, you have seen the Father. The
two are one.

"I will sing to the Lord, for He has triumphed gloriously! The horse and its rider He has thrown into the sea! The Lord is my strength and song, and He has become my salvation; He is my God, and I will praise Him; My father's God, and I will exalt Him. The Lord is a man of war; the Lord is His name." (Exodus 15:1-3)

If you are still having trouble with this concept, I suggest you turn to the book of Revelation and get a glimpse the Warrior King named Jesus Christ. There is no victory without a battle. There is no conquering king who has never gone to war. Our distaste for war does not change the facts. We have a dedicated enemy who has declared war against us. Satan is his name, and he has three main strategies: to steal, to kill, and to destroy. When an enemy declares war on you, you no longer have the luxury of a choice. You are at war. The only choices are to fight and win or give up and perish or be enslaved. Our God is not willing to let that happen. He will win and He wants you and me in the winner's circle with Him.

Shortly after bringing Israel out of Egyptian bondage, God began to refer to them as an army. I can only imagine how humorous this sounded to their enemies, who were looking at a ragtag mob of former slaves wandering aimlessly in the wilderness. But God had a plan, and His plans always succeed. Remember the words of Proverbs 19:21, NIV,

"Many are the plans in a man's heart, but it is the Lord's purpose that prevails."

"The Lord foils the plans of the nations; he thwarts the purposes of the peoples. But the plans of the Lord stand firm forever, the purposes of his heart through all generations. Blessed is the na-

tion whose God is the Lord, the people he chose for his inheritance." (Psalm 33:10-12, NIV)

"The Lord Almighty has sworn, 'Surely, as I have planned, so it will be, and as I have purposed, so it will stand.'" (Isaiah 14:24, NIV)

God's plans are clearly outlined in Numbers, chapters 9 through 13, where we see the Lord taking command of His army as He prepares them for war. One of the first tasks in training soldiers is to instill immediate obedience. Unless soldiers can respond quickly and under the control of their leaders, they will not be able to succeed in battle. So one of the first training strategies is called "drill and ceremonies." Most people who have served in the military have vivid memories of marching for many hours as they learned to quickly obey the specific commands until it became natural to obey first and ask questions later. I remember the challenge this presented to many soldiers. During one training period, the leaders required those who had difficulty with left and right turns to carry a brick in their left hand. When the command, "column left" or "left face" was called, the sergeant would quickly tell that solider to turn toward the brick. After holding the brick between their thumb and fingers (with gravity pulling it downward) for a few minutes, it began to feel very heavy. By the end of a training session, every moment holding the brick felt like an eternity of intense pain. Soldiers quickly learned to make the correct turns to avoid carrying the brick.

In Numbers, chapter 9, God begins doing "drill and ceremonies" with His army.

"At the command of the Lord the children of Israel would journey, and at the command of the Lord they would camp; as long as the cloud stayed above the tabernacle they remained encamped." (Numbers 9:18)

As they learned to respond to this training, Moses summed it up like this:

> *"At the command of the Lord they remained en-camped, and at the command of the Lord they journeyed; they kept the charge of the Lord, at the command of the Lord by the hand of Moses."*
> (Numbers 9:23)

In addition to seeing that the people had learned to follow the commands of the Lord, we also see that, like a good military leader, God delegated authority to subordinate leaders and the people learned to obey Moses as well.

An essential element of war is "command and control." When fighting breaks out, soldiers and military units experience what is known as the "fog of war." In the heat of battle, it is easy to lose communication with the command element, resulting in a greatly reduced ability to respond to the changing situations on the battlefield. In Numbers, chapter 10, we see God setting up a system of command and control.

> *"And the Lord spoke to Moses, saying: 'Make two silver trumpets for yourself; you shall make them of hammered work; you shall use them for calling the congregation and for directing the movement of the camps.'"* (Numbers 10:1-2)

These trumpets would not only send clear commands to the army, but would also be a signal to God to come to their assistance.

> *"When you go to war in your land against the en-emy who oppresses you, then you shall sound an alarm with the trumpets, and you will be remem-bered before the Lord your God, and you will be saved from your enemies."* (Numbers 10:9)

In addition to the trumpets, God used "standards" like modern day "military guidons" which are used for controlling troop movements. Each tribe had a unique standard, and all the members of the tribe knew to follow that standard into battle or during peacetime troop movements.

> *"The standard of the camp of the children of Judah set out first according to their armies; over their army was Nahshon the son of Amminadab. Over the army of the tribe of the children of Issachar was Nethanel the son of Zuar. And over the army of the tribe of the children of Zebulun was Eliab the son of Helon."* (Numbers 10:14-16)

This section of Numbers chapter 10 goes on to list how all the 12 tribes moved out by their standards under subordinate leaders. The organization of the Lord's army is becoming more and more visible and begins to look like any well-trained military force. This section is summarized as follows:

> *"Thus was the order of march of the children of Israel, according to their armies, when they began their journey."* (Numbers 10:28)

Moses and the tribal leaders of the various armies were all under the ultimate control of God. God had His own signaling system: the cloud by day and the pillar of fire by night. The leaders kept watch for the signal from God and moved quickly in obedience.

> *"Now it came to pass on the twentieth day of the second month, in the second year, that the cloud was taken up from above the tabernacle of the Testimony. And the children of Israel set out from the Wilderness of Sinai on their journeys;*

then the cloud settled down in the Wilderness of Paran. So they started out for the first time according to the command of the Lord by the hand of Moses." (Numbers 10:11-13)

A key to successful command and control is to have an established order of march. This plan was given by God and executed by Moses and the tribal leaders. Each time they moved, they were rehearsing for the day of war. Sometimes they remained in one place a very long time. At other times they were only there for one day. Can you imagine the discipline required to set up the tabernacle and all the tents for just one day? Can you picture the grumbling (common to all soldiers) when they had to break camp after such a short period of rest? But this was all building discipline and military readiness. The Lord knew that the challenges upon entering the Promised Land would be great and the people needed to be ready to meet all obstacles and enemy situations.

In chapters 11 and 12, many problems common to all military units were experienced by this newly formed army. They didn't like the food that God provided and the soldiers grumbled. The mixed rabble (non-Hebrews who came out of Egypt with them were notorious for complaining) grumbled and many Israelites joined in various small rebellions. All of this had to be dealt with now rather than during the heat of battle. It was not pretty and we often choose to skip these parts. However, they are very instructive for those who plan to be a part of God's great end time army. Learn the lessons now and avoid hardship later. It is possible to learn from the mistakes of others, and it is much less painful than making all the mistakes yourself. A part of the discipline of soldiers is to study, even if the topic is unpleasant at the time. It is amazing how often these painful lessons turn out to be the key lessons later.

Like any good leader, Moses learned to use every resource available to him. He used his father-in-law as a scout because

Hobab knew the land and all the key places for movements and establishing base camps. He sent out spies at the command of the Lord to scout out the land. His instructions to them are almost identical to current military methods of making an estimate of the enemy's situation. Everything in these four key chapters of the book of Numbers closely follows the commonly accepted elements and principles of war.

At this point, you may be wondering what all of this has to do with being valiant. Valiant soldiers are well trained, highly disciplined soldiers who trust their leaders. Valiant soldiers have a greater commitment to the whole group than to themselves as individuals, and are willing to face the possibility of death to protect their fellow soldiers and to accomplish the ultimate goals of their people. I intentionally placed the protection of fellow soldiers first because of many reports by heroic individuals who stood up to extreme danger primarily to protect their friends.

Those who desire to serve the Lord well are advised to accept their appointed leaders, the highest standards of training, and the personal discipline of a good soldier. Paul urges the church to practice good order and discipline:

> *"For God is not the author of confusion but of peace, as in all the churches of the saints."* (1 Corinthians 14:33)

Begin now by listening carefully to the guidance of the Holy Spirit. Let Jesus be your Lord and be obedient to the directives of the Holy Spirit. Be willing to follow all His commands, even if it means being quiet while He speaks through another anointed servant. Good soldiers (valiant soldiers) always put the mission before their personal needs.

Another important practice for those who would be valiant in their service to the Lord is to sincerely pray for boldness. Those who would serve well must show unusual courage under fire. Many people who wear the name "Christian" have never shared their faith in Jesus Christ with anyone who was not already a believer. Fear can prevent us from being faithful in our calling as disciples of our Lord. When we fail to share our faith in Jesus with unbelievers, it is most often because of a deep seated cowardice in our spiritual lives. We may be afraid of criticism or accusations of religious fanaticism. Some have truly bought into the more socially acceptable pattern of political correctness. We may begin to believe we are being very sensitive toward others and actually showing kindness. But what kindness is there in letting someone spend eternity in hell because we didn't openly share our faith and help them to develop a saving relationship with Jesus Christ? Remember the courageous prayer of the disciples in Acts 4:

> *"'Now, Lord, look on their threats, and grant to Your servants that with all boldness they may speak Your word, by stretching out Your hand to heal, and that signs and wonders may be done through the name of Your holy Servant Jesus.' And when they had prayed, the place where they were assembled together was shaken; and they were all filled with the Holy Spirit, and they spoke the word of God with boldness."* (Acts 4:29-31)

With great power, God answered their prayer for boldness. That power came with such force that the house where they were meeting was shaken. I think they were shaken too. Fear was shaken off of them, and courage was shaken into them. The report that follows is an inspiration:

> *"And with great power the apostles gave witness to the resurrection of the Lord Jesus. And great grace was upon them all. Nor was there anyone among them who lacked; for all who*

*were possessors of lands or houses sold them,
and brought the proceeds of the things that were
sold, and laid them at the apostles' feet; and
they distributed to each as anyone had need."*
(Acts 4:33-35)

God gave them much more than just courage. He showered them with grace. His provision was so great that not one of them was in lack. They were inspired to walk in great generosity, which resulted in everyone having their needs met. God is so faithful to provide more than we ask or even imagine.

In addition to praying for wisdom, the truly valiant followers of Jesus Christ pray for wisdom to know what to say and what to do in the appropriate moment of time. They begin to realize at a very deep level that Spirit-directed actions yield the greatest results; always bringing success to those who follow. So where do you get that wisdom? You pray for it and receive it by faith.

*"If any of you lacks wisdom, he should ask God,
who gives generously to all without finding fault,
and it will be given to him."* (James 1:5)

*"I keep asking that the God of our Lord Jesus
Christ, the glorious Father, may give you the
Spirit of wisdom and revelation, so that you may
know him better."* (Ephesians 1:17, NIV)

To all of these add your prayers for strength, ability, and skill to serve the Lord well. David reminds us that God trained his arm for battle so that he could bend a bronze bow. God will also provide strength and ability to all who ask. Here are a few scriptures to remind you of the faithfulness of God in always providing what you need.

"He gives strength to the weary and increases the power of the weak." (Isaiah 40:29, NIV)

"The Lord gives strength to his people; the Lord blesses his people with peace." (Psalm 29:11, NIV)

In 2 Chronicles, chapter 20, there is an amazing and inspirational account of an embattled people who rose up in faith and valor to march out against a much superior army. The army they faced was made up of a three nation coalition. God had forbidden Israel to attack these people or take their land because they were also descendants of Abraham. To Jehoshaphat and his people, this seemed very unfair. How could people they had sought peace with turn on them and attack with such force in an attempt to annihilate them? So they went to God and made their case. They had been obedient to the Lord and now they were in grave danger. God responded to their prayers through Jahaziel, a little known prophet who was a descendant of Asaph.

"And he said, 'Listen, all you of Judah and you inhabitants of Jerusalem, and you, King Jehoshaphat! Thus says the Lord to you: "Do not be afraid nor dismayed because of this great multitude, for the battle is not yours, but God's. Tomorrow go down against them. They will surely come up by the Ascent of Ziz, and you will find them at the end of the brook before the Wilderness of Jeruel. You will not need to fight in this battle. Position yourselves, stand still and see the salvation of the Lord, who is with you, O Judah and Jerusalem!" Do not fear or be dismayed; tomorrow go out against them, for the Lord is with you.'" (2 Chronicles 20:15-17)

Then an amazing thing happened. They accepted the word of Jahaziel without question. They were given a very interesting strategy. They were told that they didn't have to fight. All they had to do was suit up and show up. They were told to come up to their position in the battle lines, stand still and see God win the victory for them. I like that kind of outcome in battle, but can you imagine the difficulty we would have convincing a military force or a church today to follow this strategy? The sad truth is that we don't find much of this kind of courage today. We cannot find many in our nation or in any nation who see our battles as God's battles. This is considered to be a foolish and archaic worldview that doesn't embrace affirming every other religion as equal to faith in our living, creator God. But the absolute truth is that there is only one God, and He is Lord of all of creation. Consider this promise:

> *"For this is what the Lord says—he who created the heavens, he is God; he who fashioned and made the earth, he founded it; he did not create it to be empty, but formed it to be inhabited— he says: 'I am the Lord, and there is no other.'"*
> (Isaiah 45:18, NIV)

God proclaims 12 other times in scripture, "I am God, and there is no other." It may not be politically correct, but it is the absolute truth. And the battle in Jehoshaphat's day and many others in the Bible affirm this truth, and the outcome is always the same. God is a valiant warrior who does not lose any battles.

> *"So they rose early in the morning and went out into the Wilderness of Tekoa; and as they went out, Jehoshaphat stood and said, 'Hear me, O Judah and you inhabitants of Jerusalem: Believe in the Lord your God, and you shall be established; believe His prophets, and you shall pros-*

per.' And when he had consulted with the people, he appointed those who should sing to the Lord, and who should praise the beauty of holiness, as they went out before the army and were saying: 'Praise the Lord, For His mercy endures forever.' Now when they began to sing and to praise, the Lord set ambushes against the people of Ammon, Moab, and Mount Seir, who had come against Judah; and they were defeated." (2 Chronicles 20:20-22)

I love this battle plan. Pick your best worship team and send them ahead of the troops singing praise songs. I believe the members of this praise team were truly valiant in their service for the Lord. They led the charge using a method never tried or tested in the past. They bravely moved out, singing in absolute trust that God would do what He said He would do. Where are these worshippers today? We need to recruit and train more worship warriors in our churches today. And check out the results of following God's battle plan.

"So when Judah came to a place overlooking the wilderness, they looked toward the multitude; and there were their dead bodies, fallen on the earth. No one had escaped. When Jehoshaphat and his people came to take away their spoil, they found among them an abundance of valuables on the dead bodies, and precious jewelry, which they stripped off for themselves, more than they could carry away; and they were three days gathering the spoil because there was so much." (2 Chronicles 20:24-25)

Are you ready to sign up, suit up, and show up for battle today? The Lord is still looking for a few good men and women who will put their trust in Him, understand the times, recognize that we are at war, and be valiant in His service. In Psalm 110, David prophesied of the coming battle and that the followers of Jesus Christ would indeed be valiant. He said,

> *"Your troops will be willing on your day of bat-*
> *tle. Arrayed in holy majesty, from the womb of*
> *the dawn you will receive the dew of your youth*
> [or, *your young men will come to you like the*
> *dew*]. (Psalm 110:3, NIV)

Remember His promises and place your trust in Him. Hear His words and promises in scripture. Over 300 times He has called us to "fear not" because we know He is with us.

> *"Fear not, for I am with you; Be not dismayed,*
> *for I am your God. I will strengthen you, Yes, I*
> *will help you, I will uphold you with My righ-*
> *teous right hand."* (Isaiah 41:10)

> *"The Lord will march out like a mighty man, like*
> *a warrior he will stir up his zeal; with a shout he*
> *will raise the battle cry and will triumph over his*
> *enemies."* (Isaiah 42:13, NIV)

You may be wondering what being valiant has to do with entering the Secret Place. Have you noticed in the scriptures that it is the valiant people, who face great challenges requiring extraordinary courage, who speak about the Secret Place? It seems that these are the ones who hunger and thirst for it the most, and who are welcomed by God into His place of intimacy where He can provide counsel and might.

Remember, you were born in enemy territory. Since your birth (whether you realized it or not), you have been at war because your enemy has three known purposes: to steal, to kill, and to destroy. You have no choice about whether you will have war or not. When the enemy declares war on you, you are at war. The choice before you is: will you be valiant in your fight for the Lord or will you be led captive by the enemy?

The Lord calls those who stand bravely against the enemy to join Him in the Secret Place; the place of His counsel and guidance. The Lord calls those who stand with Him to come into the intimacy of His love and grace. The Lord calls those into His presence who are willing to take a stand for Christ, even in enemy territory. Remember the words of Jesus recorded in Revelation, Chapter 2:

> *"I know your works, and <u>where you dwell, where Satan's throne is</u>. And you hold fast to My name, and did not deny My faith even in the days in which Antipas was My faithful martyr, who was killed among you, <u>where Satan dwells</u>. But I have a few things against you, because you have there those who hold the doctrine of Balaam, who taught Balak to put a stumbling block before the children of Israel, to eat things sacrificed to idols, and to commit sexual immorality. Thus you also have those who hold the doctrine of the Nicolaitans, which thing I hate. Repent, or else I will come to you quickly and will fight against them with the sword of My mouth. He who has an ear, let him hear what the Spirit says to the churches. To him who overcomes I will give some of the hidden manna to eat. And I will give him a white stone, and on the stone a new name written which no one knows except him who receives it."* (Revelation 2:13-17)

As you persist in your valiant service of the Lord, you will face many challenges to your faith. But remember the repeated admonition of the Lord to be of good courage and not be afraid.

Fear does not come from the Lord. It comes from the enemy.

"For God has not given us a spirit of fear, but of power and of love and of a sound mind." (2 Timothy 1:7)

Faith is the gift of God which will support us in the face of every danger and in every time of need. Take faith and remember the words of Psalm 91:

"He who dwells in the secret place of the Most High shall abide under the shadow of the Almighty. I will say of the Lord, 'He is my refuge and my fortress; my God, in Him I will trust.' Surely He shall deliver you from the snare of the fowler and from the perilous pestilence. He shall cover you with His feathers, and under His wings you shall take refuge; His truth shall be your shield and buckler. You shall not be afraid of the terror by night, nor of the arrow that flies by day, nor of the pestilence that walks in darkness, nor of the destruction that lays waste at noonday. A thousand may fall at your side, and ten thousand at your right hand; but it shall not come near you." (Psalm 91:1-7)

"Through God we will do valiantly, for it is He who shall tread down our enemies." (Psalm 60:12)

PRAYER

"'Now, Lord, look on their threats, and grant to your servants that with all boldness they may speak your word, by stretching out your hand to heal, and that signs and wonders may be done through the name of your holy Servant Jesus.' And when they had prayed, the place where they were assembled together was shaken; and they were all filled with the Holy Spirit, and they spoke the word of God with boldness." (Acts 4:29-31)

CHAPTER 5

VISITATION IS VITAL

"So I say to you, ask, and it will be given to you; seek, and you will find; knock, and it will be opened to you. For everyone who asks receives, and he who seeks finds, and to him who knocks it will be opened. If a son asks for bread from any father among you, will he give him a stone? Or if he asks for a fish, will he give him a serpent instead of a fish? Or if he asks for an egg, will he offer him a scorpion? If you then, being evil, know how to give good gifts to your children, how much more will your heavenly Father give the Holy Spirit to those who ask Him!" (Luke 11:9-13)

During the writing of this book, my wife and I attended two back-to-back conferences. One of the things I missed most on our trip was our worship room and the type of worship we practice in our home on a daily basis. At the conferences, the music was usually loud and busy, and I found it difficult to get positioned to wait quietly on the Lord. In our worship room, we can switch from loud and energetic to soft and mellow music. We have control to shift with the movement and leadership of the Holy Spirit. As we move with Him and submit to His leadership, we can actually tangibly feel the presence of God and it is very common to have angels present in the room.

It seems very natural to move from His presence in our room to my presence in His Secret Place. During these moments with Him, I receive so much revelation. He makes Himself known and reveals so much of His desires for His people.

On one particular Friday morning, in the Secret Place, God gave me a short vision which had a profound effect on my perception of the relationship between sound and our ability to sense His presence. One sound is not better than another. One volume level is not more holy or more spiritual than another. What I experienced gave me a better understanding of the importance of our willingness to follow His leadership.

In the vision, I was on an attack helicopter flying above the clouds with the side doors wide open. A door gunner next to me was manning a large caliber machine gun. The crew was trying unsuccessfully to shout over the roar of the engine and popping sound of the rotor. Outside was a beautiful scene of white, puffy clouds floating gently under the deep blue skies above us. I had a sense that there was a beautiful silence in the atmosphere just outside the noisy helicopter, but the noise of the helicopter and its occupants prevented me from hearing the quiet I so earnestly sought. I felt like the Lord was urging me to enter a quiet time with Him, but my surroundings were blocking me from experiencing His presence.

Most of us have very busy lives and we produce so much noise. This seems like the norm for our fast-paced lifestyles and it can carry over into our worship. Some of it is true worship, but much of it seems like noise which drowns out the silence necessary to hear the still, small voice of the Lord. Sometimes I love a loud and energetic praise service. At other times, I like a quiet moment with the Lord. When the Lord begins to move and make His presence felt, I like to be able to shift and get in sync with what He is doing. I want to do whatever it takes to move from where I am into the presence of the Lord where He is waiting in secret for me to arrive. I am always hungry for Him and desire to be with Him in the Secret Places as often as I am allowed.

As I mentioned earlier, on my second visit to the Secret Place beyond the ancient door, I was led through the cloud in the first room and up the stairs behind the throne of God. On this visit, at the top of the stairs, there was an opening to a beautiful blue sky filled with stars and light, puffy clouds. It was an awesome sight. My heart longed to be in the presence of God. So I lifted my hands toward the stars in worship and cried out to God, "Lord, please come down and be in our midst! Help us to deal with some of the struggles in our world!" To my total surprise, I immediately heard a resounding, "**NO!**" In stunned silence, I listened as the Lord said, "I have already done that! My work is finished! You come up here!" Then I heard a command I had never experienced before. The Lord said in a firm but loving voice, "COME UP HERE!" In sharing this experience with others, I have tried to imitate that voice, but I can't get it to come out anything like what I heard. It was a very firm command from one with great authority. It was strong, but without any sense of rebuke. Hearing this commanding voice, I had no desire other than to immediately obey.

In the past, many of us have expected God to come to us for visitation. We didn't know that we could go to His place and visit Him. When I was growing up in the church, I don't remember ever hearing a sermon on Ephesians 2:6-7,

> *"And God raised us up with Christ and seated us*
> *with him in the heavenly realms in Christ Jesus,*
> *in order that in the coming ages he might show*
> *the incomparable riches of his grace, expressed*
> *in his kindness to us in Christ Jesus."* (NIV)

No one ever suggested that I had a Biblical authority to be in heavenly places with our loving Father God. In fact, I was never taught that Jesus preached the gospel of the kingdom much more than He preached the gospel of salvation. And I certainly was not taught and didn't understand how to get to the Secret Place of the Most High. However, I am now hearing from the Lord that we are expected to go up and visit Him so we can let Him show us the incomparable riches we have in Christ Jesus.

> *"For thus says the High and Lofty One Who inhabits eternity, whose name is Holy: 'I dwell in the high and holy place, with him who has a contrite and humble spirit, to revive the spirit of the humble, and to revive the heart of the contrite ones.'"* (Isaiah 57:15)

I know that this is a major shift in thought, because I had to go through that shift on my own. To truly make the shift requires some radical openness on our part. As I have explored this scripturally for a better understanding, I encountered Ephesians 2:18, "For through him we both have access to the Father by one Spirit." This is another radical thought. We have access to the Father along with Jesus. According to this passage, this is one of the definite works of the Holy Spirit.

When we first pondered the idea of visiting the Third Heaven or the Secret Place, we probably began by asking, "How do we get there? How do we find it?" The Bible is full of clues to guide us on this adventure, and I will suggest some steps which I hope will prove helpful to you as you begin this awesome quest.

STEP 1: YOU MUST SPEND TIME IN QUIET EXPECTATION.

Jesus taught us to connect with God in the secret place when we are praying. He said:

> *"But you, when you pray, go into your room, and when you have shut your door, pray to your*

*Father who is in the secret place; and your Fa-
ther who sees in secret will reward you openly."*
(Matthew 6:6)

Jesus emphasized that we need to get into a private place of
our own in order to meet with God in His Secret Place. There
are so many distractions around us and so much noise. Things
in the natural and things of the flesh will always distract us
from our attempts to be quiet and still in His presence. We need
to find a way to have more of these quality visits with the Lord
on a daily basis. It may not be easy. It may not always be con-
venient. So we have to sort through our priorities and decide
how we will frame our time. As for me, I will find a time and
place at whatever cost. This is just too precious to miss.

God must think it is important, because He mentions the
Secret Place so many times in the Bible. Do you know how
many times the Bible mentions the Secret Place? I will share a
few passages with you. You can search for others on your own.

*"He made darkness His secret place; His canopy
around Him was dark waters and thick clouds of
the skies."* (Psalm 18:11)

*"For in the time of trouble He shall hide me in
His pavilion; In the secret place of His tabernacle He shall hide me."* (Psalm 27:5)

*"You shall hide them in the secret place of Your
presence from the plots of man."* (Psalm 31:20)

*"You called in trouble, and I delivered you; I
answered you in the secret place of thunder."*
(Psalm 81:7)

"He who dwells in the secret place of the Most

High shall abide under the shadow of the Almighty." (Psalm 91:1)

"But you, when you fast, anoint your head and wash your face, so that you do not appear to men to be fasting, but to your Father who is in the secret place; and your Father who sees in secret will reward you openly." (Matthew 6:17-18)

With all these references, it seems clear that God is making an important point. If it is that important to Him, shouldn't it be that important to us? So I will ask again, "Have you found His Secret Place?" Have you found your Secret Place? If not, keep pressing in to find it. Remember: the Holy Spirit was given with the express purpose of guiding you into all truth. This is part of the truth. Ask the Holy Spirit to guide you in finding your entrance to the Lord's Secret Place so that you can meet with Him. He is faithful and will not disappoint you.

STEP 2: TRUST HIM. DON'T GIVE UP QUICKLY.

Waiting on the Lord involves time and perseverance. It helps to explore the journeys taken by some of those who have gone before and learn the lessons they shared. Isaiah learned a great deal about waiting on the Lord during his years of service as a prophet.

"Have you not known? Have you not heard? The everlasting God, the Lord, the Creator of the ends of the earth, neither faints nor is weary. His understanding is unsearchable. He gives power to the weak, and to those who have no might He increases strength. Even the youths shall faint and be weary, and the young men shall utterly fall, But those who wait on the Lord shall renew

their strength; They shall mount up with wings like eagles, they shall run and not be weary, they shall walk and not faint." (Isaiah 40:28-31)

Waiting on the Lord brings us into connection with His glory, power, wisdom, strength and perseverance. In this process of waiting, patience is a primary virtue, and trusting the Lord is essential. In this time of waiting, we are open to receive revelation knowledge. Psalm 46:10, "Be still, and know that I am God." This is a form of knowledge which goes far beyond mere information. In this knowledge, we are certain about who He is. And we become certain that He is faithful. We know that He has always done what He has promised, and that He will always do what He promises. This experience of knowing in the spirit is about building a relationship with the God of Heaven and Earth. This is about an intimacy with the Supreme Being we have been authorized to know as Abba, Daddy, or Papa. Wow!

STEP 3: ASK THE SPIRIT TO GUIDE YOU INTO ALL TRUTH

"But when he, the Spirit of truth, comes, he will guide you into all truth. He will not speak on his own; he will speak only what he hears, and he will tell you what is yet to come." (John 16:13, NIV)

This concept is a challenge for many people. They believe that Jesus said it, but don't really believe that it will happen for them. In the past, people have told me this only means we are enabled to know what we need to know in the Bible. I believe that this is partially correct, but it doesn't go far enough. Scripture is only truly revealed when it is discerned in the spirit through the inspiration of the Holy Spirit.

But I believe Jesus meant more than this. He was letting the disciples (then and now) know that God's Holy Spirit would come and dwell in us and teach us from the inside out. I believe that this is one of the most untapped spiritual resources available to believers. We are living in a day spoken of by the prophet Paul. We see a church that has a form of religion but denies the power. Too often, the church is so busy trying to establish and enforce doctrine that it becomes little more than a revised legalistic system. Having been set free from the law, many work diligently to quickly establish another legal system. This leads to many abuses and tends to limit the work and flow of the Holy Spirit. The church is often so busy pronouncing the "H" word (heresy) over people and ministries that it loses the very important concepts of love, grace, long-suffering, and restoration.

This is one of the reasons for God sending the Holy Spirit to us and offering the gift of discernment. It takes the pressure off of us. We are not solely responsible for maintaining the purity of thought in the body of Christ. We are not the sole source of accurate knowledge about the Bible and all things religious. When we get free from laboring over these things, we can spend more time promoting the message of love.

It is vital that we cease confessing the words of the enemy. We stand in agreement with the enemy when we become the accusers of the saints. Instead of pouring over our manmade doctrines to find heresy in others, we need to be seeking the truth from the Holy Spirit for our own lives and ministries. It is time to take a break. Let God be the judge. He is so much better at it than the wisest among us, and He is always able to temper it with love and grace. We should be in the restoration business rather than the judgment and condemnation business. Remember Paul's words of wisdom, "Knowledge puffs up, but love builds up." (1 Corinthians 8:1, NIV)

As we begin to place ourselves under the tutelage of the Holy Spirit, we become the students and He is the teacher. As in all educational settings, it is important to ask questions, and we need to be very specific about what we ask. Framing questions is an important skill for any disciple. Don't generalize about what you are seeking. It is a human defense mechanism to be general in questioning. We do it so that if we are caught asking something inappropriate, we can stand on a plea of plausible deniability. The more specific we become, the more responsible we are for the nature of the questions. Be willing to be admonished as well as blessed. There is often more learning available in admonishment than pious half truths of praise.

In seminary, I had a professor who used his own book as a text book. He repeatedly asked us to be critical of his book as a way of promoting better learning. I made the mistake of thinking he really meant it. As it turned out, he really meant that we should constantly praise his book as the definitive answer on this topic. After a moment of truth (from my perspective) with him, I found myself being considered a threat by my teacher. After this confrontation, (from his perspective) I could do nothing right in the class. I paid with a grade point for believing that he really wanted criticism. I learned a very expensive and valuable lesson: very few people are able to handle criticism. What most people really mean is for us to give them abundant praise.

In our relationship with God, we need to remember that He admonishes those He loves. Discipline, admonishment and correction are all signs of God's love for us. It is not meant to hurt us, but to get us focused on the right things. He is not trying to hurt us. He is doing what is most helpful for us. His correction is often humbling, and it can help to keep us oriented on being a blessing to others.

> "*My son, do not despise the Lord's discipline and do not resent his rebuke, because the Lord disciplines those he loves, as a father the son he delights in.*" (Proverbs 3:11-12)

This verse always reminds me of another important truth. If

you don't get admonished, be concerned! Has the Lord found you resisting His instruction? Has the Lord found you to be a mocker or a fool? Remember the clear lesson of Proverbs 9:8 (NIV), "Do not rebuke a mocker or he will hate you; rebuke a wise man and he will love you." We need to be wise and open to receive every rebuke the Lord gives.

STEP 4: ASK THE SPIRIT WHAT MESSAGE IS COMING FROM HEAVEN TODAY

This has been one of the most profound revelations I have received from the Holy Spirit. We are actually encouraged by the Lord to ask, to seek, and to find. God is not trying to hide His plans and purposes from us. He wants us to know and to understand what He expects from each of us. There is no mystery here, and even if there is a mystery, the Holy Spirit will reveal it. *Mystery* in the New Testament refers to a truth formerly hidden, but now made manifest. God is the revealer of truth, and the Holy Spirit has been sent out into all the world to guide us into all truth. Often we act as if His mission is to guide us into a few truths, but Jesus said, "All truth!" We need to accept it and start acting on it. We need to seek it with sincere hearts and truly expect to receive everything the Lord is willing to give to us.

The next step in this process is to trust that we can hear what Heaven is saying on a daily basis. If we are not hearing, it is not because the Holy Spirit has failed in His mission. It is because we have let the worries and concerns of this world veil us from the truth. It is because we are too focused on ourselves and not focused enough on God. I found over and over—in going through the process of receiving these messages and writing this book—that I experienced times of being overly concerned about what people would think of me. When I got caught up in wondering if people would think I had lost my mind or if I became concerned about accusations of heresy, it was difficult for me to hear from God. It was difficult to be open to the truth coming through the Holy Spirit when my mind focused on what people might say. We must escape from the fear of man to experience all that God has for us.

Another important revelation for me was, "Don't try to live on yesterday's revelation." The revelation of yesterday may not fit today's issues, challenges, or problems. We need a fresh revelation every day. I consider these revelations to be bread for my spirit and soul. I unashamedly ask for fresh bread from Heaven every day. Jesus said that He is the Bread of Heaven, and I want that bread daily. I like bread when it is fresh. Even the fragrance of fresh bread draws me closer to Him. We need to build that kind of hunger and develop that kind of relationship with the Holy Spirit. So that we can get daily updates. We need to be reading from the *Heavenly Times* fresh off the press in Heaven rather than (or at least in addition to) the yellow journalistic papers of the day.

Remember: don't be afraid to ask. Meditate on what Jesus meant in John 16:24,

> *"Until now you have asked nothing in My name. Ask, and you will receive, that your joy may be full."*

It is far better to ask for abundance (even if you only get part of it) than to ask for nothing and receive it all. I pray every day, "Holy Spirit, tell me what Heaven is saying today."

STEP 5: LEARN TO SEE WITH YOUR SPIRITUAL EYES

> *"Son of man, you dwell in the midst of a rebellious house, which has eyes to see but does not see, and ears to hear but does not hear; for they are a rebellious house."* (Ezekiel 12:2)

Many people tell me they want to see spiritual things, but it just isn't happening for them. After asking a few questions, I have found that most of them are still trying to see with their physical eyes. This is a very common challenge for believers. Through years of public education, most of us have been thoroughly trained to focus on the physical world. We have learned the so called "scientific method" in the laboratories of our higher institutions of learning. According to this method, the only things which are true are the things which can be verified by the five senses. Those who are well-trained in this system of thought find it difficult to accept anything not readily verifiable with the natural senses. People who hold rigidly to this world view are only willing to receive in the natural, and often reject outright anything received with their spiritual senses.

> *"However, we speak wisdom among those who are mature, yet not the wisdom of this age, nor of the rulers of this age, who are coming to nothing. But we speak the wisdom of God in a mystery, the hidden wisdom which God ordained before the ages for our glory, which none of the rulers of this age knew; for had they known, they would not have crucified the Lord of glory. But as it is written: 'Eye has not seen, nor ear heard, nor have entered into the heart of man the things which God has prepared for those who love Him.' But God has revealed them to us through His Spirit. For the Spirit searches all things, yes, the deep things of God."* (1 Corinthians 2:6-10)

A few years ago, I noticed that as I was singing the wonderful worship song, "Open the Eyes of my Heart," I was consistently singing with my eyes closed. The first time I noticed this, it struck me as odd that I would close my eyes while asking for my eyes to be opened. At first, I was a little embarrassed by this, because I was usually in front of the church when this happened. I tried to keep my eyes open, but they would automatically close as I changed my focus to the message of the song. Then it dawned on me that this was very appropriate, because I was asking to see with the eyes of my spirit rather than with my natural eyes. The best way for that to happen is for my physical eyes to be closed. Closing my eyes then became an intentional part of my prayers when singing this song. I quit trying to see the spiritual with the physical.

> *"And Elisha prayed, and said, 'LORD, I pray, open his eyes that he may see.' Then the LORD opened the eyes of the young man, and he saw. And behold, the mountain was full of horses and chariots of fire all around Elisha."* (2 Kings 6:17)

Whether in song or prayer, consider asking the Holy Spirit to help you open your spiritual eyes. Ask that you be enabled to see in the spirit realm in order to know what the Holy Spirit is doing, to see angels, and to be aware of enemy spirits working to oppose you. Paul even went further by praying that God would open his spiritual eyes to see the hope of his calling, the riches of his spiritual inheritance, and the great power of God at work in his life and ministry.

> *"I pray also that the eyes of your heart may be enlightened in order that you may know the hope to which he has called you, the riches of his glorious inheritance in the saints, and his incomparably great power for us who believe."* (Ephesians 1:18-19, NIV)

STEP 6: LEARN TO HEAR WITH YOUR SPIRITUAL EARS

An equally challenging task for those thoroughly trained in and committed to scientific methodology is to hear with their spiritual ears. However, I want to assure you that you can hear with your spirit, in your spirit, and through your spiritual ears. This is not something you train yourself to do. It is a definite spiritual gift as Paul taught in 1 Corinthians 12:7-8,

> *"But the manifestation of the Spirit is given to each one for the profit of all: for to one is given the word of wisdom through the Spirit, to another the word of knowledge through the same Spirit."*

This ability to hear comes through the indwelling Holy Spirit. We are told in 1 Corinthians 14:1 to earnestly desire spiritual gifts, and especially to prophesy. The only way we can be enabled to do this is through the gift of hearing in the spirit through the work of the Holy Spirit. It is always appropriate for us to ask for gifts and revelations which will build up, strengthen, encourage and comfort the Lord's people.

If your spiritual ears have not been opened, then it is an appropriate time to press in beyond the flesh with an earnest desire for this spiritual gift. If you are able to hear a little with your spiritual ears, it is a good time to press in and ask for more. Lord, help us to hear more of your words and more of your loving messages for others. Remember the story of Elisha in 2 Kings. In addition to being able to see in the spirit realm, Elisha was able to hear in that realm as well.

> *"And the man of God sent to the king of Israel, saying, 'Beware that you do not pass this place, for the Syrians are coming down there.' Then the king of Israel sent someone to the place of which*

the man of God had told him. Thus he warned him, and he was watchful there, not just once or twice. Therefore the heart of the king of Syria was greatly troubled by this thing; and he called his servants and said to them, 'Will you not show me which of us is for the king of Israel?' And one of his servants said, 'None, my lord, O king; but Elisha, the prophet who is in Israel, tells the king of Israel the words that you speak in your bedroom.'" (2 Kings 6:9-12)

I have experienced this gift several times in the past as people have plotted rebellion in the church. The Holy Spirit allowed me to see them in their homes and hear exactly what they were saying. This was given so that I might be prepared when the actual attack came. The Lord has provided so much for us that we have never drawn upon. If you have been gifted to minister in the prophetic, seek an increase in your anointing and the sharpening of these gifts in your ministry. If you have not received these gifts, then continue to earnestly desire them and pursue them with passion. Remember that 1 Corinthians 14:1 begins by advising us to first pursue love. God can only give these powerful gifts in the measure that we have the love to use them in accordance with His will. Make it your first priority to increase in the area of love so that God can trust you with more.

As with all physical talents and abilities, you need coaching and training in the use of spiritual gifts. You may find a wise and experienced counselor or mentor who can help you with developing spiritual gifts. That is good. However, remember that the best teacher in the use of spiritual gifts is the one who gives them. Learn to let the Holy Spirit guide you in the proper use of your spiritual ears. The Lord commanded through Isaiah, "Hear, you deaf; and look, you blind, that you may see." (Isaiah 42:18) The Lord would not give such a command if He had not already sent the giver of the gift and the teacher to guide you.

STEP 7: ASK THE HOLY SPIRIT TO TELL YOU THE MEANING OF YOUR VISIONS AND DREAMS

I want to encourage you to get over one of the biggest hurdles right now, if you haven't already done so. For some reason, many people are reluctant to ask for spiritual gifts. As a man, I have always had difficulty asking for directions when driving. I grew up with strong messages that men know these things without asking. I tend to try everything else first. So I am very grateful for the invention of GPS navigation systems. Now I don't have to ask, and I usually get to the right place at the right time.

In the same way, many people (men and women) hesitate to ask the Holy Spirit for the gifts they need in ministry. They try everything else first. I want to assure you that it is okay to ask. In fact, our Lord specifically told us to do so in Luke, Chapter 11:

> *"So I say to you, ask, and it will be given to you; seek, and you will find; knock, and it will be opened to you."* (Luke 11:9)

When you ask, you are in fact being obedient to the Lord. So I encourage you to ask every time, as soon as you see a need. Ask as soon as you feel a desire to go deeper in your relationship with the Holy Spirit and deeper in your gifting for service.

It is not offensive to God for you to want to understand. The entirety of the Bible testifies to this truth. God actually spoke most of the Torah to Moses so the people could understand His plan for their lives. God spoke through the prophets so people would understand His strategies and purposes for them. God spoke through Jesus Christ to make it abundantly clear to us that He loves us and wants to reveal Himself to us. Jesus taught and modeled this truth.

"Jesus said to him, "Have I been with you so long, and yet you have not known Me, Philip? He who has seen Me has seen the Father; so how can you say, 'Show us the Father'?" (John 14:9)

I believe that it is offensive to leave the Lord's presence not knowing anything. In that same verse (John 14:9), Jesus seemed amazed that He could have been with them for three years, and they still didn't understand who He was. When we spend time with the Lord in the heavenly realms, we should never return as we were before. Spending time in His presence should result in a renewed mind, a transformed soul, and a glowing countenance. That renewed mind should be filled with understanding and knowledge of who He is and what He plans for us.

On my first throne room visit, I was so amazed that I felt totally stunned. I couldn't speak. I could barely move. And I asked nothing. The next day I received a teaching about asking the Holy Spirit to tell us the meaning of the things we see in visions and dreams. That night, I prayed to go back to that same spot so I could ask a question that was burning in my mind. I was immediately taken back to the same spot. At first, I was caught in stun mode again. I thought I had a question, but I couldn't remember what I wanted to ask. After what seemed like a very long time, I remembered my question. Then, after catching my breath and getting my composure back, I asked my question. I spoke gently and respectfully, "Your Word says that I am seated with you in heavenly places. I would like to know where to find my seat." Jesus turned toward me with a very loving smile on His face and motioned with His hand for me to be seated. I was already positioned at my seat when I asked, and I have been in that same spot every time I have visited that room. Ask and you shall receive.

STEP 8: GETTING TO KNOW THE VOICE OF THE SHEPHERD

"I am the good shepherd; and I know My sheep, and am known by My own. As the Father knows Me, even so I know the Father; and I lay down My life for the sheep. And other sheep I have which are not of this fold; them also I must bring, and they will hear My voice; and there will be one flock and one shepherd."
(John 10:14-16)

In the spirit realm, it is critically important to know who is speaking. The enemy tries to counterfeit everything that the Lord does. If the Lord speaks to you, the enemy will try to imitate His voice and speak to you. He will say something that is contrary to the Word of the Lord or that will bring confusion into your spirit about the meaning of God's Word. So you must know who is speaking. Is it the Lord, the enemy, or your own sensual nature? Jesus doesn't leave us defenseless before the enemy. He declared, "My sheep hear My voice, and I know them, and they follow Me." (John 10:27) We need to be constantly talking with the Lord so that we immediately know His voice and do not follow another.

When federal agents are being trained to identify counterfeit money, they are not taught to recognize every different type of counterfeit currency. They are taught to recognize the real thing. If you have studied and know the real thing totally, you will never accept something that is counterfeit. If you know the real thing, you will immediately recognize the difference. So many different methods of counterfeiting have been used that it is not possible to know all of them, but you can know the real thing. In the same way, if we study the voice of the Lord and know it thoroughly, we will not be fooled by the enemy's attempt at deception.

The Lord is so good to us that He doesn't stop there. He has given us another method of testing to know the source of spiritual direction. We must ask ourselves: "Does it line up with the Word of God?" The Holy Spirit will never direct you to do anything contrary to the written or spoken Word of God. Test each thing you hear against what the Word says. Of course, this means that you have to have a thorough knowledge of the Word. This is not an odious task as some have assumed. Those who love the Lord also love His Word and spend as much time as possible studying it.

A third method is to ask: "Does it line up with the known will of God?" The most frequently asked question during many years of ministry has been, "How can I know God's will for my life?" It really isn't a great mystery. It has been written down and in print for centuries. As you study the Word, pay close attention to those things which are stated to be the "will of God." You may be amazed at how clear it is. I shared this idea in one church and the pastor looked it up. He found 312 references to the will of God. Again, to know the Word of God requires that you regularly spend time in study.

God is so good to provide even more ways to determine if it is the voice of the Lord. Begin with this question, "Are there other spirit-led, mature witnesses who can assist in validating this message?" If you have a mentor or mature advisor, go to that person and ask for his or her input. Remember what Paul taught about confirming things through other witnesses.

"By the mouth of two or three witnesses every word shall be established." (2 Corinthians 13:1)

A final test is: "Are you in agreement with others?" Has the Lord revealed this same message to other trusted sources? Has the Lord given another mature believer an experience similar to this? Are you standing in agreement on this issue? There is great spiritual power in agreement. We must learn to use it wisely and well.

STEP 9: YOU MUST DEVELOP THE HABIT OF JOURNALING

This was a difficult lesson for me to learn. It took a long time for me to develop the discipline of journaling. I have talked with so many people who have had dreams, visions, and Third Heaven visits, but have forgotten the details of what God wanted them to learn. They didn't write it down, and as their memories faded some of it became distorted. The best way I have found to prevent forgetting key lessons or distorting the story over time is to journal, and go back to the journal each time you have an opportunity to tell it, teach it, or write about it. I have a written journal for all the key messages from the Lord, as well as recorded messages for many of these experiences.

One of the most exciting outcomes for me in journaling was to discover that the Holy Spirit continues to guide you as you write. I have prayed for this many times, because I don't want to lose the edge on any of these lessons from the Lord. As you journal, open your spirit to go deeper with the Holy Spirit, and ask Him to continue to reveal the truth to you. If you begin to journal something you do not yet understand, ask the Holy Spirit at that very moment to reveal it to you. He is so faithful and so good to teach, guide, and empower us to do the will of the Father.

Journaling provides numerous opportunities to ask for the deeper meaning of signs, images, symbols, and words of instruction. Take every opportunity to ask what these things mean. As you prayerfully journal, revelation can continue to unfold as you write. If you are receiving it from the Holy Spirit, you do not have to worry about adding something to the original visit or revelation. Pause occasionally, as you journal, to meditate quietly on each idea. Continue to do this until you have pulled every last morsel from every part of the event.

Another frequently asked question is, "What if I only received a little image or experienced a short vision?"

Remember the advice of <u>Zechariah 4:10</u>, "For who has despised the day of small things?" Rejoice and celebrate everything the Lord provides for you. Nothing He does is ever wasted or out of proportion to His will. You could write an entire book from some of the very brief pictures you receive in a vision. There is an old saying, "A picture is worth a thousand words." With the Holy Spirit, begin to expand on the picture and watch the words and meanings flow into you and through you.

If thanksgiving is the way through the gates, it is also the way to gain permission for a return trip to Heaven. Don't despise even the very smallest of beginnings. Rejoice that the Lord has spoken to you and stir up an expectation that there will be more. Begin to expect much so that much more will be coming your way very soon. Get excited and thankful about small things to open the way for the larger things of God.

STEP 10: YOU MUST BE FREE FROM UNFORGIVENESS & STRIFE

Even though I have saved this point for last, it is actually a first priority. Because it is so important, I saved it for now so that it will be most fresh on your mind after you finish reading this chapter. You simply cannot be in His presence filled with unforgiveness, bitterness, or strife. These three emotions can find no place in Heaven with the Lord. Some people are just unwilling to let these emotions go, but I assure you that the price for holding onto them is just too high. I don't want any-thing to interfere with my opportunities to visit the Lord in Heaven. Whatever it is, I know the price is too high if it keeps me from that intimate relationship with the Father, the Son, or the Holy Spirit. Carefully consider the cost and decide what you will choose to do.

I believe that forgiveness is a choice and not a feeling. We can choose to forgive, whether our feelings are in agreement or not. We can choose to forgive over and over until the feelings match the decision. Remember, we walk by faith and not by feelings. We don't have to be controlled by our emotions or some false sense of what is just or right in this world. We can follow the example of our Lord and bless those who desire to do us harm. Paul summed it up like this: "Bless those who persecute you; bless and do not curse." (Romans 12:14) Consider carefully what Paul is saying to the Roman church. I see so many people living lives in opposition to God who believe that all these emotions are acceptable to Him. Dear friends, this cannot be! We must rid ourselves of all such things if we want to spend time with the Lord. Be concerned about the consequences of living in opposition to the will of God.

> *"And even as they did not like to retain God in their knowledge, God gave them over to a debased mind, to do those things which are not fitting; being filled with all unrighteousness, sexual immorality, wickedness, covetousness, maliciousness; full of envy, murder, strife, deceit, evil-mindedness; they are whisperers, backbiters, haters of God, violent, proud, boasters, inventors of evil things, disobedient to parents, undiscerning, untrustworthy, unloving, unforgiving, unmerciful; who, knowing the righteous judgment of God, that those who practice such things are deserving of death, not only do the same but also approve of those who practice them."*
> (Romans 1:28-32)

Did you notice where strife is listed in this passage? It is right in between murder and deceit. Paul considers strife to be among the very worst offenses. Yet, so many who consider themselves to be Christ's disciples seem to enjoy causing strife everywhere they go. They don't seem to be convicted by it or even consider it something to be dealt with quickly. Some have been so thoroughly given over to it that they believe there is something holy about causing strife in the body of Christ. They act as if they are called to a ministry of strife and are proud of the degree to which they have developed their gift. However, the Lord will not allow this in His presence. You simply cannot spend time with Him in Heaven if you haven't dealt with strife. So purge your heart before asking to enter the Secret Place! Remember the words of Psalm 24,

> *"Who may ascend into the hill of the Lord? Or who may stand in His holy place? He who has clean hands and a pure heart, who has not lifted up his soul to an idol, nor sworn deceitfully."*
> (Psalm 24:3-4)

Work diligently to keep your heart pure and your hands clean.

WHEN GOD INVITES YOU TO AN APPOINTED TIME, DON'T MISS IT!

In these challenging times, we need a fresh revelation every day, and I believe it is the Lord's will to provide it for us. God simply does not expect us to live and work in spiritual darkness. God is the great revealer of mysteries. He wants you to know what He expects of you. He wants you to know the plan and purpose He has for your life. He wants you to understand that He has planned good things for you and He is not trying to harm you.

> *"'For I know the plans I have for you,' declares the LORD, 'plans to prosper you and not to harm you, plans to give you hope and a future. Then you will call upon me and come and pray to me, and I will listen to you. You will seek me and find me when you seek me with all your heart.'"*
> (Jeremiah 29:11-13, NIV)

118

In these last days, one of our primary tasks is to prepare the bride for His return. Preparing and adorning the bride requires great wisdom and revelation. The Lord has not deserted us or left us to our own designs. He is still very much engaged with His bride. Some have taught that all the gifts of the Spirit were for a previous time and only for a few select people. However, when Paul wrote the first letter to the Corinthian church, it was well past the time some have declared the gifts to have expired. Why would Paul urge us to seek something that God had no intention of giving? Why would he spend an entire chapter teaching the proper use of gifts if they are no longer available? Do we seriously believe we serve a God who would dangle these delicacies before us and then refuse to give them to His children? That isn't the loving God that I serve. Believe, seek, and find all that God has for you.

> *"Pursue love, earnestly desire spiritual gifts, and especially that you may prophesy!"* (1 Corinthians 14:1, paraphrased)

This is serious business with God. He wants to prepare you to be a kingdom carrier. He wants you to spread the kingdom far and wide. He wants you to bring others into the kingdom. With these tasks, He is offering the gifts you need to accomplish your mission. Don't waste your time or His time trying to search out ways to argue with His plan or bring more strife to the body of Christ. Go to the Word and find that all of this is clearly described in His scriptures, and begin to operate in it now.

Use your Biblical authority to visit the place in Heaven where you have already been seated.

> *"You were seated with Him in heavenly places."* (Ephesians 2:6, paraphrased)

Use your Biblical authority for access to the Father along with Jesus Christ by the same Spirit that opened the way for Him. If you have access to the Father, where do you suppose He is right now? He is in Heaven right now, and you have a promise that you can be with Him through the work of the Holy Spirit.

> *"For through Him we both have access by one Spirit to the Father. Now, therefore, you are no longer strangers and foreigners, but fellow citizens with the saints and members of the household of God."* (Ephesians 2:18-19)

You are a fellow citizen with the saints. This is your passport to the Secret Place and the heavenly realms. You are a member of the household of God. Do you honestly believe that the Father refuses to let family members into His house? That is not a description of the Father God I love, worship, and serve. Begin to see Him as He really is. When you see His glory, you see His goodness. And it is goodness that He has planned for you.

> *"Let us therefore come boldly to the throne of grace, that we may obtain mercy and find grace to help in time of need."* (Hebrews 4:16)

Where do you suppose this throne of grace is located? According to the writer of Hebrews chapter 4, it is located in Heaven with Jesus. The only way we can fulfill this challenge is to appear before the throne of grace in Heaven, now. Now is when we need the benefits of His grace. Consider one more scriptural authority to approach His presence with boldness which comes from being in Christ and covered with His righteous acts:

"Therefore, brethren, having boldness to enter the Holiest by the blood of Jesus, by a new and living way which He consecrated for us, through the veil, that is, His flesh, and having a High Priest over the house of God, let us draw near with a true heart in full assurance of faith, having our hearts sprinkled from an evil conscience and our bodies washed with pure water." (Hebrews 10:19-22)

PRAYER

Father God, I praise you for your goodness. I stand in awe of your love, patience, and long suffering on our behalf. I thank you that you have loved us so much that you have invited us to be with you in heavenly places. Papa, I pray for all who are reading this book to find their own way into the Secret Place of the Most High—that place of intimacy with you. Daddy, I am praying to you as a loving Father to allow all of your sons and daughters to have Third Heaven experiences. Father God, I pray for their spiritual eyes to be opened wide, their spiritual ears to hear clearly, for their hearts to be receptive, and for their minds to be renewed as they spend time in your presence. I pray for the renewal of their minds to bring about a transformation of their souls. Papa, I ask you to help them, through the work of the Holy Spirit, to be freed from unforgiveness, bitterness, and strife so they will be fitted by you to come into your presence. Father God, I pray that kingdom carriers will be birthed in the Spirit today, and together we can bring your kingdom on Earth as it is in Heaven. I pray for your will to be done on Earth as it is in Heaven. Papa, give each of them an open Heaven experience and let them hear your call, "COME UP HERE!" I pray all these things in accordance with your Word and in the precious name of *Yeshua ha Messiach*! Amen and Amen!

CHAPTER 6

GETTING A VERTICAL PERSPECTIVE

"Then Jesus answered and said to them, 'Most assuredly, I say to you, the Son can do nothing of Himself, but what He sees the Father do; for whatever He does, the Son also does in like manner. For the Father loves the Son, and shows Him all things that He Himself does; and He will show Him greater works than these, that you may marvel.'" (John 5:19-20)

"I can of Myself do nothing. As I hear, I judge; and My judgment is righteous, because I do not seek My own will but the will of the Father who sent Me." (John 5:30)

During a Friday night worship service, I was caught up into the Third Heaven for a lengthy period of time. As the service began, I was unaware that the pastor was ill that evening. He called an elder after the worship started to inform him of his illness and his plan not to attend the service. The pastor asked the elder and the worship leader to handle the service, but they were not sure what they should do. They decided to continue the praise and worship part of the service until an inspiration came. As a result, the praise portion of the service lasted almost two hours instead of the usual one hour. This was very unfortunate for the pastor, but it gave me an extra hour in the Third Heaven. This extended visit in Heaven resulted in one of my most awesome and informative experiences ever.

That night I saw the 10,000 times 10,000 and thousands of thousands of angels singing praise to God. Have you considered how many angels that could be by doing the math? The smallest number would be 104,000,000 angels, and it could actually be many more than this. As I looked in amazement, I could see more and more angels gathering around Father God. It seemed like it would never end as the number grew larger and larger. As they sang and released their praise, they glowed with the glory of God. They looked as if they were on fire and a powerful, amber-colored glow lit up all of the area around them. With all these fiery angels glowing, Heaven was very bright that night. That night I became more fully aware of how the angels respond to human worship. They get energized by the whole-hearted praise of dedicated worshippers and begin to give more and more glory to God. It is not always like that in Heaven. I have seen the angles looking bored during some services and extremely intense and energized by others. It all depends on the quality and sincerity (not volume) of our worship and praise.

Father God was in a very good mood that night and the Shekinah glory danced around and over Him and His throne. At one point, the cloud of His glory extended upward and then moved over to me. I was literally lifted up in that amazing blue/purple cloud which seemed to be dancing over the Father. Enveloped by the cloud, I was actually dancing over the Father. I was totally thrilled by this experience. The blue cloud was warm and comforting, and I felt such a wonderful peace. Then Father God said, "And you have always wondered why you loved the color blue!" I instantly knew that I had sought that cloud of His presence all of my life without fully understanding its nature. I was suddenly filled with revelation and understanding which covered my entire lifetime. So many things from my past quickly came into proper spiritual perspective, and I understood for the first time how all of these experiences were woven together to reveal my heart's desire to be with Him forever. This moment of intense revelation gave me such a deep sense of peace, love, and acceptance. It is beyond words to explain this life-changing moment in Heaven. One simple sentence along with the guidance of the Holy Spirit brought it all together for me. I am still in awe of what He can suddenly do with our lives.

As I was returned to my seat in Heaven (which is near the throne of Jesus), I continued to watch in awe as the cloud danced over and around Father God. I was not fully prepared for what happened next. Suddenly, Father God responded to the praise in Heaven and on Earth with a wave of power that almost crushed me. It is difficult to describe this wave since we have nothing like it on Earth. It is like an intense power pulse from God that goes all the way through you. It is made up of a combination of His energy, love, life, and awesome power. It felt incredibly wonderful, even though I was being crushed by it. It was so good that I cried out, "More, more, more!" Then the Father said to me, "You cannot take more! You are still in the body and you will perish from more of this power!" I began to consider what He said. At that moment, I knew my heart's desire and was ready to cry out, "Go ahead and do it! Give me more, and then I can just stay here." Before I could voice this desire, there were two more waves similar to the first, but slightly less intense. I felt so alive, totally healed, extremely blessed, and full of life, joy, and love. I just wanted to stay there forever. I did not want to leave.

In this short time in Heaven, I experienced a peace beyond anything I have ever known. I had no other place to be. I had no appointments, no schedules, and no phone calls to answer. There were no church services or board meetings to attend. There were no emergencies or calls to rush to the hospital. There were no memorial services or funerals to plan and conduct. I was completely free from worry, anxiety, and stress. I was where I was supposed to be and there was nothing to even compare with the importance of this moment. I didn't want to give it up. I just wanted to be with Him, worship Him, dance with Him, sing with the angels, and give Him all the glory forever and ever without end. In that moment, nothing else seemed important by comparison.

At what seemed like a great distance from where I was located, I heard the worship leader speaking. I was aware that my body was still in the church, but my spirit was totally in Heaven. I was able to sense both places in the spirit, but the place on Earth seemed so distant and so detached from the real me. (I shared a portion of this experience in Chapter 3.) The worship leader cried out something about the power of the devil and how we could overcome it in worship. I was amazed at the response in Heaven. The angels in Heaven also heard the cry of the worship leader. They all looked around at one another and asked, "Who?" I immediately understood what they meant. The devil is not even a memory in Heaven. In this place he has no power, no influence, no meaning, no value, no purpose, and no presence. This is a place where we can be completely free from him forever. That was a moment of awesome revelation. I knew this in my head, but now my spirit knew it, too. My perspective on spiritual warfare was totally transformed in that moment. I moved to a greater grasp of the spiritual authority the Lord has given us. I remembered what Jesus said to His disciples, and now I understood it more fully than ever before. I also understood completely that this was also a promise for me.

> *"And He said to them, 'I saw Satan fall like lightning from heaven. Behold, I give you the authority to trample on serpents and scorpions, and over all the power of the enemy, and nothing shall by any means hurt you.'"* (Luke 10:18-19)

Worship in Heaven continued, and I was filled with joy and peace beyond anything I have ever known. Then I heard the church elder speaking in the distant church service, and I knew it was almost time for me to return to the earthly realm. However, I honestly didn't want to leave. I cried out, "I don't want to leave!" Then I heard the Spirit say, "You don't have to! You can be here and there at the same time." It was then that I had another profound revelation about the words of Jesus from the fifth chapter of John. Jesus said that He only did what He saw the Father doing and He only said what He heard the Father saying. He was able to do this because He was aware of both Heaven and Earth at the same time. I was filled with joy that I was experiencing something similar to that, and I was overjoyed at the promise that this could continue after I returned to my body in the natural realm. I wondered what that might be like as I slowly rejoined the service in progress at the church. As I looked at the leaders and the people, I could see Heaven, the Lord, the angels, the 24 elders, and all of the heavenly host. It was an awesome and awe-inspiring experience. I wondered how long it would last. I didn't want to lose this very precious gift from the Lord.

For several weeks, I was able to see Heaven and Earth at the same time during most of the day each day. After a few months, I experienced it only as I focused spiritually and as I pressed in to experience it more fully. After several more months, this is still possible when I focus on the Spirit Realm.

This experience in Heaven was such a strong reminder of our need to keep a vertical perspective. Most of the time, we are focused on the natural and we often miss what is happening in the spiritual. This is not God's plan for those who are citizens of the kingdom. God's desire is summed up fairly well in 2 Corinthians 3:18,

*"But we all, with unveiled face, beholding as in
a mirror the glory of the Lord, are being trans-*

formed into the same image from glory to glory, just as by the Spirit of the Lord."

You may be struggling with doubt about whether or not you can experience this in your own spiritual walk. I am convinced that you can, and that it is God's desire for you. I believe that this is the reason God asked me to write this book. He wants you to know that it is His desire for you to have similar experiences with ever-increasing intensity.

I began to wonder why more people do not experience these types of Third Heaven visits. I believe it is because we have been trained so thoroughly in the natural while our spiritual training has been very lacking. We need teachers who have had these experiences to begin to lead the children and youth to a much higher level of functioning in the kingdom of God. We need teachers who will help people understand that the spiritual realm is actually more real than the natural and will last much longer. The things which are natural will pass away, but the things which are spiritual will last for all eternity. We need to give more attention to the things which are permanent and focus less on the things which are passing away.

To see the things of the Spirit, you must use your spiritual eyes. Too many people are straining to see with their physical eyes. This is to be expected because, as I said above, we have all been thoroughly trained in the natural. We have learned to believe what we can experience with our five senses, and to distrust anything that cannot be validated by our own experience and reason. While this training may help you in your daily living and in the academic realm, it is not the highest reality. As a beginning point, try to remember that seeing does not lead to the highest experience of believing. In the spiritual realm, believing is seeing, and you accept these realities on faith and wait (free from anxiety) until they manifest in the physical realm. We must learn to "walk by faith and not by sight."

> *"But, how will they learn unless someone is will-ing to teach?"* (Romans 10:14, paraphrased)

This is what the Lord has called me to do. Take a few moments to read and meditate on the definition of faith in Hebrews 11:

> *"Now faith is the substance of things hoped for, the evidence of things not seen."* (Hebrews 11:1)

So how can faith be substance and evidence? In the nat-ural, this just doesn't make sense. We have been taught that seeing is believing and that we can trust (have faith) in what we can already see, hear, touch, taste, and smell. But faith in what we have already seen or received by our five senses is not faith at all. So we have to make a choice: Do we walk by faith or will we walk by sight? I choose both with clear parameters. When I am walking, driving, eating, and etc., I choose to use my five senses. When I am doing scientific research, I believe in what I can see and demonstrate for others to experience. God created these natural abilities for us in order to help us live in the natural world. We would be foolish to deny them. Serious injury can come from dis-obeying the laws of nature.

However, the Lord also created us to live in the spiri-tual world. If we fail to use the skills and abilities He has provided for this part of our experience, it is as foolish as driving a car blindfolded with our ears plugged. It is simply unwise to use the wrong skills in either setting. Therefore, we need to develop spiritual flexibility and wisdom in our choices. To experience the heavenly realms, you must learn to walk by faith and not by sight. You must learn to believe and then wait to see. You must trust the promises of the Bible and believe that you actually do have spiritual eyes and ears. You must believe that you can see and hear in the Spirit. If you ask for these things, but do not believe that you will receive them, you are double minded and you should not expect anything.

> *"If any of you lacks wisdom, let him ask of God, who gives to all liberally and without reproach, and it will be given to him. But let him ask in faith, with no doubting, for he who doubts is like a wave of the sea driven and tossed by the wind. For let not that man suppose that he will receive anything from the Lord; he is a double-minded man, unstable in all his ways."* (James 1:5-8)

At this point, I want to discuss some spiritual realities, but I am limited to the natural realm of paper, words, and concepts. So I am going to ask you to bear with me as I attempt to explain the next point from a spiritual perspective. The first statement I want to make is: "The flesh only sees horizontally." Now, in the natural this is not true. You can look up and see vertically and you can lower your eyes and see horizontally. However, for this discussion, I want to use the term *vertical* to mean the spiritual realm and *horizontal* to mean the physical realm. So please bear with me as I place some limitations on the meaning of these two words.

That first statement ("The flesh only sees horizontally.") is meant to say, "your physical eyes can only see in the physical world." In order to see in the spiritual realm, most of us must learn to close our natural eyes in order to see. You may have a gift for open visions where you are participating in a vision with your eyes open. But for most people (at least in the beginning), it is helpful to keep their physical eyes closed while they are attempting to look into the spiritual realm. This may be difficult in the beginning, but you can ask the Holy Spirit for help. So, the first step is to learn to close the eyes of your flesh as you use the eyes of your heart (spirit).

If you see a faint or vague image, go with it. As your spiritual skills and seer abilities increase, things will become clearer to you. If you are concerned about whether this is real or your imagination, ask the Holy Spirit. Jesus promised,

> *"However, when He, the Spirit of truth, has come, He will guide you into all truth; for He will not speak on His own authority, but whatever He hears He will speak; and He will tell you things to come."* (John 16:13)

I believe that what Jesus meant when He said "all truth" was ALL TRUTH. This includes answering our questions about the things we experience in the spirit. I have come to rely on and trust this ministry of the Holy Spirit in all things spiritual.

Those trained to operate in the gifts of the Spirit, especially the prophetic, have been taught to understand there are at least three possible sources for the words of knowledge we receive. These words may come from God, from the enemy, or from our own spirit. It is important to know which source is behind any prophetic word. So how can you know for sure? You ask the Holy Spirit, who has been assigned to you so that He can guide you into all truth. You check it out in the Word of God. You will never receive a message from God that contradicts His Word. The same is true in every area of the spiritual realm. Ask and you will receive. After a little training and experience, you will come to know His voice. If you can't recognize His voice in words of knowledge and words of wisdom, you probably will not know it in any other area of your faith walk. Trust in the teachings of Jesus! Believe what He says in His Word and in your spirit.

> *"But you do not believe, because you are not of My sheep, as I said to you. My sheep hear My voice, and I know them, and they follow Me."* (John 10:26-27)

Listening for and hearing the Lord's voice will assist you in maintaining a vertical perspective. Many church goers only spend a few minutes a week focusing vertically on the things of Heaven. When the scriptures are read, they have a brief moment of focus on heavenly realities. When the sermon is preached, they have an additional opportunity to focus on God's perspective. During praise and worship, many believers have their spiritual eyes open briefly to get a glimpse of the realms of Heaven. Unfortunately, when church is over, many shift their focus away from the things of Heaven and back on the natural things of this world until the next church service. They are like those Jesus described in the parable of the sower.

> *"This is the meaning of the parable: The seed is the word of God. Those along the path are the ones who hear, and then the devil comes and takes away the word from their hearts, so that they may not believe and be saved. Those on the rock are the ones who receive the word with joy when they hear it, but they have no root. They believe for a while, but in the time of testing they fall away."* (Luke 8:11-13, NIV)

Some believers who are more deeply spiritual than others still struggle in this dimension, because they have no idea how to establish and maintain a vertical perspective. During times of intense worship or focused meditation, they clearly have a vertical perspective. They are able to see and experience the deep things of God for brief periods, but lack the ability to maintain that focus for frequent or long periods of time. The things of this world draw their attention away from Heaven, and they are drawn back by the cares of the world.

> *"The seed that fell among thorns stands for those who hear, but as they go on their way they are*

choked by life's worries, riches and pleasures, and they do not mature." (Luke 8:14, NIV)

Much of our time, by necessity, has to be focused on the things of this world. We have personal needs that must be met. We must have food, shelter, and clothing to survive. If we want to live well and provide for our families, we have to be focused on jobs, careers, financial planning, and the myriad of other concerns which seem necessary in our modern world. In addition to these basic human needs, we also have social needs which must be met. We are also aware of having many family needs which cannot be ignored. The Lord knows all these things, and His Word acknowledges the need for church leaders to have good family relationships.

> *"Here is a trustworthy saying: If anyone sets his heart on being an overseer, he desires a noble task. Now the overseer must be above reproach, the husband of but one wife, temperate, self–controlled, respectable, hospitable, able to teach, not given to drunkenness, not violent but gentle, not quarrelsome, not a lover of money. He must manage his own family well and see that his children obey him with proper respect. (If anyone does not know how to manage his own family, how can he take care of God's church?)* (1 Timothy 3:1-4, NIV)

People who follow Jesus Christ still have jobs or businesses which must receive adequate time and energy to be successful and fruitful. Kingdom-focused businesses not only provide income for the owners, workers, and their families, but also produce financial resources for ministries, missionaries, and churches. Owning, operating, or working in a kingdom business requires you to spend time focused on the horizontal dimension. If you own a kingdom business, you need to also keep the vertical focus operational in order to follow the vision and plans of the Lord. It requires spiritual wisdom to keep a proper balance between your focus on work and keeping your eyes fixed on Jesus.

In addition to our family and business focus, we have friendships which require time to develop and maintain. Many people come to accept Jesus as Lord and Savior through their friendships with other believers. We also have opportunities to lead others to Christ after we have built solid friendships based on trust. This is one of the most effective tools of evangelism. Our ultimate purpose is in the vertical, but many of the actions and activities which maintain friendships must—by necessity—be oriented toward the natural. We first appeal to the natural desires for supportive and helpful relationships and then lead them to the vertical relationship with our Father God and our Lord Jesus.

Ironically, much of our church activity is actually on the horizontal plane as we focus on the business side of the church. Buildings must be maintained, updated, remodeled, and cleaned on a regular basis. Mortgages have to be paid and funds for new construction and programs must be raised and properly handled by responsible stewards. Activities must be planned, organized, and conducted with sufficient attention to detail to produce the desired results while avoiding financial mismanagement. While we are doing many good things, we can easily slip into the habit of neglecting the most important thing—our relationship with God. This is a particular challenge for many senior church leaders who—by necessity—have to spend a great deal of time in planning, programming, coordinating, and overseeing activities, while maintaining a healthy worship and devotional life.

When I speak of maintaining a vertical perspective, I am not denying any of these needs. I simply believe that we have the ability to spend more time on our vertical relationships than most of us are doing now. The real challenge is in establishing and maintaining an appropriate and spiritually healthy balance. As you properly plan for meeting your commitments to family, church and friends, continuously plan for time to spend with the Lord. If this is a real priority in your life, it will begin to occupy space in your day planner. Specific times and places will be planned and programmed for the purpose of having face time with the Lord.

If you desire Third Heaven visitation, you must see this as a priority. You can't just drop in occasionally and pick up where you left off. God is not running vacation tours to Heaven for our entertainment and pleasure. He is running the universe and He requests that His key leaders and servants spend time with Him to understand better what is expected, what is possible, and what is most efficient. Remember that the eyes of faith see both vertically and horizontally.

We need help in maintaining an upward focus, and God has not left us without the needed resources. God has provided His Holy Spirit to teach us, guide us, and keep us focused. What we need to learn is to seek the Holy Spirit's help and then be quiet and be taught.

Don't merely come to Him with a laundry list of blessings and things that you want. Come to Him to bless Him. I have talked with many people who have never considered that they are able to bless the Lord. They have been taught that the greater always blesses the lesser. The idea of blessing God seems inappropriate and even a little sacrilegious to these people. If you struggle with this, check it out in the Word of God. A good place to begin is by looking closely at the teaching of Psalm 103:

> *"Bless the Lord, O my soul; And all that is within me, bless His holy name! Bless the Lord, O my soul, And forget not all His benefits: Who forgives all your iniquities, Who heals all your diseases, Who redeems your life from destruction,*

Who crowns you with loving-kindness and tender mercies, Who satisfies your mouth with good things, So that your youth is renewed like the eagle's." (Psalm 103:1-5)

Father God wants to have a personal relationship with you. He has provided the way for you to have access to Him. Remember what Jesus said in John 14:

"If anyone loves me, he will obey my teaching. My Father will love him, and we will come to him and make our home with him." (John 14:23, NIV)

The Lord has decreed that you are His Temple. Your heart is the place where He wants to abide. If He and the Lord Jesus are abiding in you, you should feel confident that you are also welcome in His Secret Place.

"Therefore, brothers, since we have confidence to enter the Most Holy Place by the blood of Jesus, by a new and living way opened for us through the curtain, that is, his body, and since we have a great priest over the house of God, let us draw near to God with a sincere heart in full assurance of faith, having our hearts sprinkled to cleanse us from a guilty conscience and having our bodies washed with pure water. Let us hold unswervingly to the hope we profess, for he who promised is faithful." (Hebrews 10:19-23 NIV)

Did you catch that last part? "He who promised is faithful." So what is holding you back? It certainly isn't the Lord. He has invited you to get that vertical perspective and to travel in the vertical to be with Him in Heaven. All you have to do is to want that face time with Him and seek it with all your heart. Trust the Word which says, "Draw near to God and He will draw near to you." (James 4:8a)

I want you to experience something the Apostle John wrote about in the fourth chapter of the book of Revelation.

> *"After these things I looked, and behold, a door standing open in heaven. And the first voice which I heard was like a trumpet speaking with me, saying, "Come up here, and I will show you things which must take place after this."* (Revelation 4:1)

I remember very clearly the first time I heard the Lord say, "Come up here!" I have tried to imitate His voice so that others could receive it, but I simply cannot. He said the words with such command authority that I knew that my only choice was to obey. His voice was strong and powerful. Yet, the sound of His voice was also filled with love and acceptance. Only the Lord can say things so powerful and commanding in a voice filled with love. He is indeed an amazing God, and I cannot stop giving Him praise, glory, honor, and majesty for who He is and what He has done. Every visit to Heaven fills me with more awe and respect for Him.

SHIFTING TO A VERTICAL PERSPECTIVE IN PRAYER

After visiting in the Third Heaven several times, I started to notice a huge shift in the way I pray. I found that I rarely ever pray for anything for myself unless it is related to ministry. I noticed that I was no longer praying very often from a horizontal perspective. Let me explain. Prayer with a horizontal perspective usually focuses on us, our needs, our desires, our hopes, our dreams, and our plans. Many people pray as if God is writing down His "to-do list" for the day. They seem to think it is their task to fill His schedule so that He will have plenty to do and that praying fervently will result in receiving more stuff from Him. This kind of prayer started to seem like an insult to God. It started to sound like the one praying is saying, "God doesn't really know what is going on unless I tell Him." It also started to sound like I didn't really trust Him to take care of me. When I prayed for the same thing over and over, it started to feel like I needed to remind Him of things I had prayed before. All of this began to seem disrespectful toward our loving Father God.

Most of our intercessory prayers are less self-focused, but are often still only oriented toward the horizontal dimension. As with prayers to meet our own needs, requests to the Lord for other people are often focused on the things of this world. We haven't shifted to the vertical in our prayers simply because we are asking the Lord to meet someone else's needs. If these prayers are only focused on needs for the here and now, they are still horizontal. So I continued to struggle to understand how we can shift to the vertical as we intercede for others. Over time, something began to emerge. I realized that we need to ask often, "Will what I am seeking in prayer bring glory to God or to man?" I was reminded again of the teaching of Jesus.

> *"Therefore do not worry, saying, 'What shall we eat?' or 'What shall we drink?' or 'What shall we wear?' For after all these things the Gentiles seek. For your heavenly Father knows that you need all these things. But seek first the kingdom of God and His righteousness, and all these things shall be added to you."* (Matthew 6:31-33)

Every living human being has basically the same needs. God knows these needs and doesn't have to look to us for this information. He has already committed Himself to taking care of us and meeting our needs. When He brought us under the blessing of righteous Abraham, he released that seven-fold blessing to provide for us and to prosper us in every area of our lives. He will not leave us or abandon us. He will not forget us or fail to see our hardships and problems. He will always give us the good and perfect gifts from above. Remember what Jesus promised:

> *"Do not fear, little flock, for it is your Father's good pleasure to give you the kingdom."* (Luke 12:32)

How does a vertical perspective differ from a horizontal view in prayer? First, shifting to the vertical means focusing more on the Lord, rather than on ourselves. When we focus on His plans and pray for them to come to pass on Earth as in Heaven, we are praying to bring glory to God through the fulfillment of His promises. When we focus on His purposes, we are placing our trust in Him. We are praying from a position of faith. We know with certainty that His Word is true. He has a good plan for us, and He will provide what we need to accomplish His purposes in our lives, our families, and our ministries. Remember what He said to Jeremiah:

> *"'For I know the plans I have for you,' declares the Lord, 'plans to prosper you and not to harm you, plans to give you hope and a future. Then you will call upon me and come and pray to me, and I will listen to you. You will seek me and find me when you seek me with all your heart. I will be found by you,' declares the Lord."* (Jeremiah 29:11-14a, NIV)

A vertical perspective acknowledges that His goals and objectives for your life and the lives of those you love are greater than your own. His desire for your success is far greater than your own. His desire for your family is more perfect than yours. His plans and His desires for your ministry are much higher than yours. To help expand your perspective on how the Lord is providing for you and others, study and consider what James taught!

> *"Every good gift and every perfect gift is from above, and comes down from the Father of lights, with whom there is no variation or shadow of turning."* (James 1:17)

Be intentional about setting your mind on things above when you pray. You don't need to keep praying over and over for what He has already given. You need to reach out in faith and take these things rather than continuing to cry out for them. You need to build up your faith until it manifests, rather than continuing to ask for what you have already received. Paul was trying to help the Colossians understand this when he wrote:

> *"Since, then, you have been raised with Christ, set your hearts on things above, where Christ is seated at the right hand of God. Set your minds on things above, not on earthly things. For you died, and your life is now hidden with Christ in God."* (Colossians 3:1-3, NIV)

When we truly develop a vertical perspective, our prayers shift to asking for the things which will bring glory to the Lord. We become focused more on Him and less on ourselves. For many of us, we just need to get over ourselves. It is not all about us. It is about Him and His glory. We are at our best when we are focused on Him and His plan for our lives. We are at our best when we live in faith, believing that the blessing of Abraham is truly ours. When we live and pray with this perspective, the Lord opens the storehouse of Heaven and pours out more blessings than we are able to hold. In fact, He gives so much that we have to share with others.

> *"Now to him who is able to do immeasurably more than all we ask or imagine, according to his power that is at work within us, to him be glory in the church and in Christ Jesus throughout all generations, for ever and ever! Amen."*
> (Ephesians 3:20-21, NIV)

Add this prayer given by Paul to the prayers you are lifting up. It will help you to change your perspective. Think more about the last part of the prayer rather than being merely focused on the things we will receive. It is not merely about us getting more than we want. It is about giving Him the glory He so richly deserves.

Do you desire to get closer to the Lord? Do you have a passion to spend more time with Him? Do you want to have some Third Heaven visits yourself? Begin by developing a passion for Him. Build up your hunger for His presence more than His presents. Focus on who He is and what He has already done for you and others. Speak aloud your thanksgiving and praise. As you daily recite His awesome character traits, His mighty deeds in the past, the awesome things He has done for you and continues to do for you in the present, and all the things He has promised to do in the future, you will feel yourself being drawn to Him with an overflowing heart of gratitude. It is not our needs which draw us to Him. If that's all there is in your relationship with the Lord, you will pull away as soon as you get what you want. It must be so much more than this. It is in the act of falling passionately in love with the Lord that you are drawn to Him. It is the heart desire of the bride to spend more and more time with the Bridegroom. Love draws us to Him and love draws us heavenward. Love gets our attention fixed on Him, and love keeps our eyes on Him.

"But it is good for me to draw near to God; I have put my trust in the Lord GOD, That I may declare all Your works." (Psalm 73:28)

As you get closer and closer to maintaining this vertical perspective, you will find that you are more and more in sync with the Lord. You will find yourself loving what He loves, loving whom He loves, and loving yourself as He loves you. From this place of love and faith, you can begin to do some real Third Heaven intercession. It is much safer and more satisfying to do Third Heaven warfare than Second Heaven warfare. As you war in the heavens (from the Third Heaven), you can focus on others and their needs from a completely different perspective. You will begin to see people as the Lord sees them and you will be praying to lift them up to a much higher anointing than they now know. When you love people as the Lord loves them, you will desire more of those good and perfect gifts for them and your prayers will begin to release these resources from the storehouse in Heaven. When you are intentional about praying the revealed will of God over the lives of others, you will release His power to accomplish it. When you pray in the authority of Heaven, you will release the power of Heaven over their lives.

When you pray from a Third Heaven perspective, you will be very careful about what you ask for, because you now know with certainty that the things you loose on Earth will be loosed in Heaven. This promise of the Lord will take on a whole new level of meaning for you.

"Assuredly, I say to you, whatever you bind on earth will be bound in heaven, and whatever you loose on earth will be loosed in heaven." (Matthew 18:18)

PRAYER

"Therefore I also, after I heard of your faith in the Lord Jesus and your love for all the saints, do not cease to give thanks for you, making mention of you in my prayers: that the God of our Lord Jesus Christ, the Father of glory, may give to you the spirit of wisdom and revelation in the knowledge of Him, the eyes of your understanding being enlightened; that you may know what is the hope of His calling, what are the riches of the glory of His inheritance in the saints, and what *is* the exceeding greatness of His power toward us who believe, according to the working of His mighty power which He worked in Christ when He raised Him from the dead and seated *Him* at His right hand in the heavenly *places,* far above all principality and power and might and dominion, and every name that is named, not only in this age but also in that which is to come." (Ephesians 1:15-21)

CHAPTER 7

VISIONS BEING RELEASED

It was an unusually cool spring morning on Prayer Mountain above Moravian Falls, NC. We were attending a prayer meeting and had received an awesome teaching on spiritual warfare. Before opening the floor for prayer, we shared a time of praise and worship. During this time, I really got into my zone of deep spiritual worship. I was feeling the presence of the Lord and seeing small glimpses of Heaven. I felt really good in His presence. Then, I was startled by a tickling feeling on the left side of my forehead. I couldn't imagine anyone being disrespectful enough to go around tickling people with feathers, but that is what I felt. Then I felt it on the right side of my forehead. I reached up with my left hand and gently touched these places. My thumb touched the left side and my ring finger touched the right side. The tickling sensation stopped and I lowered my hand. Then it happened again. I went through three of these episodes before I opened my eyes to see what was happening. When I opened my eyes, I was startled to see an angel standing in front of me with his nose very close to my nose. I had never experienced an angelic visitation like this before, and it took a few moments to get over the surprise.

The appearance of the angel was like a consuming fire. It was awesome and powerful and it was looking me right in the eye. This was a little disarming. Then the angel spoke to me and said, "Wake up! Wake up your seer anointing! There are things you need to see in the spiritual realm!" I got the message. I had gotten caught up in the worship and was enjoying a very deep sense of personal peace. I was meeting my own needs, but things were happening which were more important than my experience in worship. I knew the angel was speaking the truth. I was not operating in my anointing as a seer, and there were things I needed to see in the Spirit. As I realized this, the angel pointed in the direction of the group. It was a large group this morning, as participants from two conferences joined with the regular attendees. Both overflow rooms were filled to capacity. However, I was seeing beyond those who were present in the room.

As I looked at the group, I was aware that I was seeing many more people than those who were seated in the room. I was seeing a spiritual truth for people around the world who are trying to follow Jesus and be led by the Holy Spirit. As I watched, I saw several dark angels (sent by the enemy) trying to wrap themselves around the heads of the Lord's people. They were trying to sit on peoples' shoulders and wrap their arms around their eyes. From this position, each of them was able to block both the person's ears and eyes. The Lord told me they had been sent by the enemy to bring a cloud of confusion over His people. Their plan was to block people from receiving what the Lord was releasing and, at the same time, steal everything the Lord had already given to His people. The Lord then let me know that this was a prophetic word for this season and for all those who are seeking to deepen their relationship with Him and for those who desire to operate with greater spiritual gifts.

At this moment, I knew the Lord was going to do something, but I didn't know what. As I continued to watch, a large number of angels came into the room. I called them angels of fire, because they all had the same fiery appearance as the angel which had awakened me from a spiritual stupor. These angels each had something which looked like a vacuum cleaner. Suddenly, they went into action and vacuumed up every dark angel in the room. However, they didn't stop with that operation. They continued to vacuum up everything left behind by these fallen angels. Every bit of residue from their work was gone in an instant. As the angels of fire completed their work, more angels of fire came into the room. These angels went to each person (whether they had been touched by the dark angels or not). They were ministering spiritual gifts, restoration, and renewed strength to everyone. The angel which had awakened me was ministering these gifts and graces to me.

In my spirit I said, "Wow! Thank you Lord! You provide for your people even before they ask! You watch over us and release power and gifts even while our minds are at rest! You break the power of the enemy, even when we are not aware of his presence! You provide for us far above and beyond what we can ask or imagine. I am feeling so overwhelmed with joy and gratitude to you; our amazing and awesome Father God! I am so thankful to our Lord, Jesus Christ, who provides more than enough! I am so thankful for the powerful presence of the Holy Spirit who gives us comfort, counsel, strength, gifts, blessing and favor every moment of every day! Lord, thank you!!!! Amen and Amen!"

After this prayer, the Lord gave me a word to minister to His people. "Be strong and courageous! You are not alone! The Lord your God is with you! The Lord your God is the keeper of His Word! The Lord your God is the keeper of His people! He is your protector, defender, and guardian! What can the enemy do to you? What can man do to you? The almighty creator God, El Shaddai, is with you! Amen and Amen!"

My mind immediately went back to Ephesians 3:20-21:

> *"Now to him who is able to do immeasurably more than all we ask or imagine, according to his power that is at work within us, to him be glory in the church and in Christ Jesus throughout all generations, for ever and ever! Amen."* (NIV)

When the Lord releases powerful visions to us, it is not

merely to make us feel good or even to elevate and bless us. It is to bring glory to God and bring glory to His church. It is His desire to release the seer anointing to all believers so that His Word can be released to the church and the world. The ultimate end result, coming from what the Lord is doing, is to increase His glory and strengthen the Body of Christ. However, I am convinced that many people do not truly believe this. They are holding onto some man-made doctrines which deny the present power of God working in and through His saints. It is time to open our spiritual ears to hear the fullness of what Peter proclaimed on the Day of Pentecost:

> *"But Peter, standing up with the eleven, raised his voice and said to them, 'Men of Judea and all who dwell in Jerusalem, let this be known to you, and heed my words. For these are not drunk, as you suppose, since it is only the third hour of the day. But this is what was spoken by the prophet Joel: "And it shall come to pass in the last days, says God, That I will pour out of My Spirit on all flesh; Your sons and your daughters shall prophesy, Your young men shall see visions, Your old men shall dream dreams. And on My menservants and on My maidservants I will pour out My Spirit in those days; And they shall prophesy."'"*
> (Acts 2:14-18)

There are more than 100 references to visions in the Bible. We are first introduced to visions in the very first book of the Bible (Genesis) and we continue to read about them all the way through to the last book of the Bible (Revelation). Many Biblical characters are mentioned by name as having been taught, guided, protected, and disciplined in visions. Abraham, Moses, Samuel, Nathan, Isaiah, Ezekiel, Daniel, Obadiah, Nahum, Habakkuk, Zechariah, Peter, Ananias, Paul, and John are all named as people who experienced visions.

In the scriptures, we see that Gentiles are also guided by visions given by the Lord. Balaam—a false prophet—had authentic visions from God, but he failed to be obedient to the revelations and came under severe judgment. Cornelius, on the other hand, was obedient to the vision and received great blessing for himself and his entire household (family members and servants—all Gentiles).

Visions were so common in Biblical days that anything out of the ordinary was thought to be a vision. Peter thought he was having a vision when the angel led him out of prison, and didn't recognize that the angel and his escape were real until he came to himself on a city street.

> *"Now behold, an angel of the Lord stood by him, and a light shone in the prison; and he struck Peter on the side and raised him up, saying, 'Arise quickly!' And his chains fell off his hands. Then the angel said to him, 'Gird yourself and tie on your sandals'; and so he did. And he said to him, 'Put on your garment and follow me.' So he went out and followed him, and did not know that what was done by the angel was real, but thought he was seeing a vision."* (Acts 12:7-9)

Growing up in so-called "mainline" churches, I never heard a message or received a lesson on the Lord guiding His people through visions. I was certainly never taught that believers today could receive and be led by visions from the Lord. Later, I was told by many church leaders and teachers that visions were only for the early church (the New Testament Church), and were no longer available to believers. These leaders taught me that all I needed to know was in the Bible and that God did not give any further revelation to individuals or to the church. Some teachers even limited this phenomenon of visions and prophecy to the 12 apostles. As I began to study the Bible in depth, I came to realize that these teachings were false. What I was being taught was not even consistent with the words of the Bible. In studying the scriptures, I found that there were 23 named apostles and references to many others in the New Testament. I discovered that there were many prophets in the early church and that prophets and prophetic words continued on into the third generation of believers. These prophets were both men and women (as Joel prophesied). I also found that many Jews and Gentiles were led by visions from the Lord.

On the day of Pentecost, Peter made the fullness of Joel's prophecy very clear.

> *"Then Peter said to them, 'Repent, and let every one of you be baptized in the name of Jesus Christ for the remission of sins; and you shall receive the gift of the Holy Spirit. For the promise is to you and to your children, and to all who are afar off, as many as the Lord our God will call.'"*
> (Acts 2:38-39)

The same thing experienced by the 120 believers in the Upper Room is available to people who are far away in distance and in time. According to Peter, this promise was and is for all who are called by the Lord our God. If you have been called of God to be a disciple of Jesus Christ, you should expect to be taught, guided, and disciplined in visions from the Lord. If you haven't received this gifts of the Holy Spirit, ask and you will receive, seek and you will find. Jesus said it so beautifully.

> *"If you then, being evil, know how to give good gifts to your children, how much more will your heavenly Father give the Holy Spirit to those who ask Him!"* (Luke 11:13)

How did the teachings of the church degenerate to the point of falsely teaching that visions are no longer available to God's people? My wife, Gloria, is quick to respond, "It is because they haven't experienced it. So they don't believe anyone else can." I call all to return to the pure teaching of the Word of God. Trust His words and lean not on your own understanding or the understanding of so-called theologians who do not know the Lord personally. What does the Lord say?

> *"Then He said, 'Hear now My words: If there is a prophet among you, I, the LORD, make Myself known to him in a vision; I speak to him in a dream.'"* (Numbers 12:6)

I believe that one part of the problem for many people in the church can be found in the word *vision* itself. This word has many different meanings in the English language. These meanings range from the ability to see with the natural eyes to seeing the supernatural with spiritual eyes. In more recent times, one particular definition has been widely used in the development of business plans in a variety of different organizations. This definition of vision has to do with the ability of astute business executives to develop a vision of the future for an organization based on statistical analysis and creative thinking. In this usage, the entire thing is a product of the creativity and wisdom of people. Many of these business models twist the meaning of Proverbs 29:18, "Where *there is* no vision, the people perish:" (KJV). The twist is to give some Biblical authority to their process of developing business models. However, this is not the intended purpose of this passage of scripture. This verse really has nothing to do with business models, even when employed by churches. This misuse of the word by churches has helped to increase the confusion over the concept of visions of the Lord and has actually led to a new level of spiritual deception. In addition, none of the current Biblical translations from the original languages use the phrase "the people perish."

In the use of this passage of scripture, it is important to keep it in the context of the original by including the verses before and after verse 18. Perhaps the best current translation of this passage is found in the English Standard Version.

> *"Discipline your son, and he will give you rest; he will give delight to your heart. Where there is no prophetic vision the people cast off restraint, but blessed is he who keeps the law. By mere words a servant is not disciplined, for though he understands, he will not respond."* (Proverbs 29:17-19, ESV)

The central teaching of Proverbs 29:17-19 concerns the disciplining of sons and servants. Without prophetic vision, people cast off restraint and position themselves to perish spiritually and—in extreme cases—they may perish physically. We see this over and over in the scriptures. When the Lord delivers people from some great difficulty and showers them with blessings, they tend to focus on the things of the flesh and cast off restraint. They are not open to receiving prophetic visions from the Lord, which come to specifically discipline or admonish them. The primary teaching of Proverbs 29 is that mere words are not enough to keep us obedient and faithful to the Lord. We need more. We need prophetic visions to confront us with the truth about our behavior and the quality of our relationships with the Lord. When we listen to and follow the guidance of the Holy Spirit, we delight the heart of the Lord. Then we are enabled to draw near to Him and to more fully understand that He desires to draw near to us.

If it is your heart's desire to enter the Secret Place of the Most High God, then you must live in a way that pleases, blesses, and delights Him. If you want to have Third Heaven visits, you must be open to the Lord's discipline and correction in order to get your heart right with Him. Our Father God knows that we can't do this on our own or by our good works. So He has made a way, paid the price, and opened the door for us to enter. Visions are intended to show us the doorway into His presence.

I believe that there are at least five steps we need to take in the area of visions.

1. SEEK A VISION

The Holy Spirit is a gentleman. He doesn't go where He is not welcome and He doesn't force gifts on those who do not want them. Jesus made this clear:

> *"So I say to you, ask, and it will be given to you; seek, and you will find; knock, and it will be opened to you. For everyone who asks receives, and he who seeks finds, and to him who knocks it will be opened. If a son asks for bread from any father among you, will he give him a stone? Or if he asks for a fish, will he give him a serpent instead of a fish? Or if he asks for an egg, will he offer him a scorpion? If you then, being evil, know how to give good gifts to your children, how much more will your heavenly Father give the Holy Spirit to those who ask Him!"*
> (Luke 11:9-13)

You may wonder why anyone would not want to have a vision. There are several reasons. For example, Job said, "Then you scare me with dreams and terrify me with visions," (Job 7:14). People who fear the judgment of God can be terrified by a vision, thinking that they are being punished. It can also be fearful to receive a vision dealing with judgment for someone else if you are the person the Lord has called to deliver the message.

Nathan had a vision from the Lord. It must have been confirming for his ministry to receive such an important message from the Lord. But then he had to give the message of judgment to someone else. He had to tell the king of Israel that he had sinned and deserved to die. It can be hazardous to your physical health to carry messages of judgment to people with great authority.

Many of the Old Testament and New Testament prophets paid the ultimate price for being faithful witnesses for the Lord. Jonah found that the price of disobedience to God was greater than the threat from man. If God gives you a prophetic message and you refuse to obey, it can be hazardous for your spiritual, as well as your physical, well-being. For those who are controlled by a spirit of fear, this may seem like a terrible double bind. Instead of casting out the spirit of fear, some people choose to willingly accept the deception of the enemy. As a result, they may choose to avoid visions altogether, hoping not to be called to carry such powerful messages to others. Remember who sends a spirit of fear to you. It is never the Lord.

> *"For God has not given us a spirit of fear, but of power and of love and of a sound mind."*
> (2 Timothy 1:7)

The truth is that God will not force you to listen. However, the consequences of choosing not to listen can be great. If we grieve the Holy Spirit, He may depart from us. If we refuse to obey God, he may hand us over for judgment and correction. I prefer to be disciplined and admonished by the Lord as soon as I need it. Then, I can make corrections in my spiritual life and stay in fellowship with Him. This intimacy with the Lord is so important to me that I pray daily to hear from Heaven what will please, bless, and honor the Lord. I want to bless Him and please Him more than I fear His judgment. I want to be in fellowship and obedience. One way to do that is to openly seek visions on a daily basis. The Lord is so faithful and good to give to those who ask; to supply those who seek, and to open to those who knock. Don't give up! Persistently seek and you will find. As you make your decision, meditate on the following two passages.

> *"Pursue love, and desire spiritual gifts, but especially that you may prophesy."* (1 Corinthians 14:1)

> *"But he who prophesies speaks edification and exhortation and comfort to men."* (1 Corinthians 14:3)

This one thing I know with certainty. I want to have every spiritual gift the Lord has for me. I want to have the Father's love in me in such abundance that I love other people as He loves them. I understand that I will only have spiritual gifts to the measure of my love. Gifts, authority, and spiritual power are very dangerous apart from His love. So I make it my goal to pursue love and desire it more than food or water. I must have His love to survive spiritually in this world. I absolutely must have it to thrive in the Spirit. From His love flows an intense desire for spiritual gifts because I must have and use them in order to please Him. I am especially focused on my desire for the gift of prophecy. It is such a powerful key to moving in accordance with His will, and it opens so many doors into the hearts and minds of others. As my last birthday approached, I did something I had never done before. I asked the Lord for a birthday gift. I asked for an increase in prophetic gifting so that I could serve Him better and minister more effectively to His people. I challenge you to earnestly desire spiritual gifts; especially the gift of prophecy.

2. TEST A VISION

During my army training, I learned how to make "sole source justifications" in order to receive the most desirable products when I placed a requisition through the military procurement system. This was the only way to assure receiving the correct products in the right quantity. Early in my time of military service, I ordered communion wine for the Catholic congregations meeting on the installation. I asked how much they needed for the year and was told that 36 bottles would meet the need. I then ordered 36 units of this product for them from a certain supply house. However, I wasn't clear enough in my description to justify this being a sole source order. The supply officer found what he thought was a cheaper source and ordered the 36 units from them. A few weeks later, I received 36 cases of the wrong type of wine. People who heard about this large delivery were quick to suggest a party. There was no party, but there was a good lesson in this experience for me. After this disaster, I always provided a strong sole source justification with all the orders I submitted.

In the spiritual realm, there is more than one source for visions and revelations. Here too, it is important to be clear with your sole source justifications. In the spiritual realm, in addition to visions from the Lord through the Holy Spirit, we may receive visions from the "familiar spirits" which are servants of the enemy. Those who are operating in the new age movement, witchcraft, or occult spiritualism use these familiar spirits as their source for visions, revelations, and fortune telling. They may sound genuine because the demonic spirits know things about people which are difficult to explain in the natural. They use this hidden information to convince people that they are genuine. The truth is that they are genuine – from a genuinely evil source. Another source for visions and prophecies is our own human spirits. Unfortunately, this information is not necessarily from the Lord and may reflect our own desires, needs, and personal issues. Words from our spirits should never be given as words from the Lord. We need to be certain of the source of any vision or revelation before taking action on it or sharing it with others. We are told in scripture to test the spirits.

> *"Beloved, do not believe every spirit, but test the spirits, whether they are of God; because many false prophets have gone out into the world. By this you know the Spirit of God: Every spirit that confesses that Jesus Christ has come in the flesh is of God, and every spirit that does not confess that Jesus Christ has come in the flesh is not of God. And this is the spirit of the Antichrist, which you have heard was coming, and is now already in the world."* (1 John 4:1-3)

The Lord spoke to Jeremiah about false visions.

> *"Your prophets have seen for you false and deceptive visions; they have not uncovered your iniquity, to bring back your captives, but have envisioned for you false prophecies and delusions."* (Lamentations 2:14)

Concerning false visions, the Lord said to the prophet Ezekiel,

> *"Her prophets plastered them with untempered mortar, seeing false visions, and divining lies for them, saying, 'Thus says the Lord GOD,' when the LORD had not spoken."* (Ezekiel 22:28)

These false prophets had spoken the outcomes they desired and then attributed them to the Lord. Their visions were false and they were subject to judgment for proclaiming them.

I do not share these warnings to prompt you to avoid visions, but to encourage you to test the spirits and be certain that they are from the Holy Spirit. John gave us the Key. Do the visions give us a true picture of Jesus? Are they in accordance with the written Word of God? Remember, God will not give you a revelation or vision which contradicts His Word. His Word is truth, and that truth will never change. However, to be able to apply the tests, you must know the Word. I encourage you to study the Word of God constantly and store it up in your heart so that you may know what is true and good and from the Lord.

3. TRUST A VISION

I will immediately put a qualifier on point number three. Trust the visions after you have tested the spirits and know with certainty that they are from the Lord. Study the three passages below as you develop your theology concerning visions and revelations from the Lord. When you put all three of these verses together, you have a fairly thorough understanding of how to test the spirits, and determine if visions and prophecies are true and from the Lord.

"The angel said to me, 'These words are trustworthy and true. The Lord, the God of the spirits of the prophets, sent his angel to show his servants the things that must soon take place.'" (Revelation 22:6, NIV)

"The law of the LORD is perfect, reviving the soul. The statutes of the LORD are trustworthy, making wise the simple." (Psalm 19:7, NIV)

"All Scripture is given by inspiration of God, and is profitable for doctrine, for reproof, for

correction, for instruction in righteousness, that the man of God may be complete, thoroughly equipped for every good work." (2 Timothy 3:16-17)

The key is knowing that it is the voice of the Lord you hear in the vision. How can you know that it is His voice you are hearing? Jesus said, "I am the good shepherd; and I know My *sheep,* and am known by My own." (John 10:14) The big question is: Do you belong to the Lord Jesus? If you are His and you are known by Him, you will know His voice because you are listening to Him daily. It is important to spend time listening to the Lord so that you will know with certainty when it is truly Him. The tenth chapter of John is an excellent place to study and prepare yourself to hear and follow His voice. Consider the following promise of the Lord:

"My sheep hear My voice, and I know them, and they follow Me. And I give them eternal life, and they shall never perish; neither shall anyone snatch them out of My hand. My Father, who has given them to Me, is greater than all; and no one is able to snatch them out of My Father's hand. I and My Father are one." (John 10:27-30)

I believe the Word of God! I believe what Jesus said! If Jesus said that I can hear His voice, I am convinced that I can do that. That is why I go before Him every day, asking to hear what He and the Father are saying in Heaven. I desire more than anything to follow Jesus, and I know from His Word that hearing His voice and knowing His voice are the keys to success. Are you listening for Him? Are you listening to Him and obeying His words?

4. TELL A VISION

One of my biggest challenges in the beginning was to build up my courage to tell others about the visions I was receiving. At first, I was afraid that people would think I was crazy or that I was trying to fool them. When the visions really began to flow, I was not around many people who had ever experienced any of these things. When the Lord told me to share some messages with others, I tried to bargain my way out of it. I told Him that I feared what people would think about me. But when I resisted, the Lord challenged me with these words, "And exactly who is it that you think you are?" It was then that I realized that what people thought of me didn't really matter very much. What really matters to me is what the Lord thinks of me. It didn't really matter very much if people rejected me along with the messages I was giving them. What really mattered was that I was willing to obey the Lord and that I was seeking to please Him by being faithful to carry out His orders. What became very important for me was for the Lord to know that He could trust me as His messenger.

We simply have to get over ourselves and realize that it is not all about us. It is about Him and what He is doing now for the sake of eternity. When I finally got the message, I was freed up to do what He asked me to do. I lost some friends, but what kind of friend refuses to accept who you are in Christ? The Lord gave me more friends who supported and blessed me. I learned that I can trust the Lord. He knows more than I know. He understands better than I am able to grasp things. Doing what He says always works. So I encourage you to trust Him. Tell others what He tells you to say.

What really surprised me were the results. Some of the most difficult messages to pass along produced the absolute greatest results. The Lord knows when people are ready to hear the truth. When we are ready to tell the truth in love (see Ephesians 4:15), the Lord will bless the messages to be fruitful in the lives of those who receive them.

At this point, I want to make a very important distinction. When you are obedient to this word, you are telling God's truth in love. I have seen so many abuses of this passage. People dump their twisted version of their truth on someone and claim that it is given in love. After hearing some of these messages, I cannot find any love in them at all. People use this as an excuse to do deep injury to others and place the blame on the Word of God. Please do not do this! When you are thinking about telling the truth, make sure it is God's truth. How do you know? You can go to His Word and validate the messages. You can ask the Holy Spirit to reveal the truth to you! You can ask Father God to give you an outpouring of His love for others so that you will always minister in accordance with that love. Remember what Jesus promised:

> *"I still have many things to say to you, but you cannot bear them now. However, when He, the Spirit of truth, has come, He will guide you into all truth; for He will not speak on His own authority, but whatever He hears He will speak; and He will tell you things to come. He will glorify Me, for He will take of what is Mine and declare it to you."* (John 16:12-14)

Jesus and the Holy Spirit are both very careful to only say the things the Father says. They do not presume to speak on their own, and we should not think we can do more than they are allowed to do. The truth they share is Father God's truth. How do we dare to do more than this? How do we dare to speak a word from our own hearts and call it God's truth? This is very serious and we need to be careful. The Lord will hold us accountable for what we say! Remember Jesus' warning to all of us:

"But I say to you that for every idle word men may speak, they will give account of it in the day of judgment. For by your words you will be justified, and by your words you will be condemned."
(Matthew 12:36-37)

If the Lord is going to hold us accountable for idle words, what will He do with words falsely attributed to Him? What will He do with words given to intentionally bring hurt to someone else in His name? If we want to be justified by our words, we must strive to speak His truth in His love all the time. If we don't want to be condemned by our words, we must be very careful about the words which come out of our mouths.

5. TEACH A VISION

During my time as an active duty Army Chaplain, I served a number of years in military hospitals and ended my time of service as the Army Medical Command Chaplain. One of the lessons I learned from the world of medical education was a very simple training model. It was shared with me as the model to train surgeons. It goes like this:

WATCH ONE
DO ONE
TEACH ONE

There is a depth of hidden wisdom in this very simple model. No matter how many books you read, nothing beats having the opportunity to watch someone else do something in a completely correct and professional way. I only finished part one of this medical model. I observed a heart by-pass procedure, but they had no intention of letting the chaplain do one. That was as far as my credentials could take me, and after that experience it was as far as I wanted to go. However, for those who desire to be heart surgeons, they must take the next step and actually perform the procedure. In some training models, this is considered the end step in the process. But there is great wisdom in point number three. When you prepare to teach a skill to someone else, you learn it in more depth than ever before. When you teach a technical procedure, you must be very careful to follow every step to the letter or the students will not learn what you want them to learn. One of my beloved military commanders was fond of saying, "If there is mist in the pulpit, there is a fog in the pew!" Teaching takes you to a higher level, and I believe that teaching is the ultimate learning experience.

This hidden wisdom is also true in the area of spiritual training. It is wise to associate with someone who is a known seer and learn from observing them. Seek out a mentor who is willing to help you learn and assist you in your understanding. But if you stop here, you will never truly accomplish the ultimate goal. You must seek the gifts and operate in them regularly in order to go higher. I have seen many people who are constantly looking for impartation of gifts, but they never actually use the gifts. They are so focused on getting more that they fail to truly activate what they have already received. I believe that every spiritual gift is activated by taking action on it. I also believe that gifts are strengthened by using them.

"For though by this time you ought to be teachers, you need someone to teach you again the first principles of the oracles of God; and you have come to need milk and not solid food. For everyone who partakes only of milk is unskilled in the word of righteousness, for he is a babe. But solid food belongs to those who are of full age, that is, those who by reason of use have their senses exercised to discern both good and evil." (Hebrews 5:12-14)

This passage confirms that exercising our spiritual senses is the key to developing them. This is a good lesson, but did you catch the desired outcome stated in this passage? The writer says that you should be a teacher by now. If you don't use the spiritual gifts (Do One), you can't progress to the teaching level (Teach One). If you stop at the middle level, you will never reach the goal of being a teacher. Remember the purpose for the five-fold offices of ministry.

> *"And He Himself gave some to be apostles, some prophets, some evangelists, and some pastors and teachers, for the equipping of the saints for the work of ministry, for the edifying of the body of Christ, till we all come to the unity of the faith and of the knowledge of the Son of God, to a perfect man, to the measure of the stature of the fullness of Christ; that we should no longer be children, tossed to and fro and carried about with every wind of doctrine, by the trickery of men, in the cunning craftiness of deceitful plotting, but, speaking the truth in love, may grow up in all things into Him who is the head—Christ— from whom the whole body, joined and knit together by what every joint supplies, according to the effective working by which every part does its share, causes growth of the body for the edifying of itself in love."* (Ephesians 4:11-16)

Everything the Lord does has a purpose. He didn't set people apart for the offices of ministry so they could be honored and have titles to put on their business cards. He set people apart for the equipping of the saints (training) for ministry and to edify the body of Christ. His purpose went further than merely conferring titles. The Lord wants us to grow up. He doesn't want us to always be children, needing someone to take care of us. We need to grow up in the faith and begin to take care of others, train them, impart to them, and let them begin to do the work of the ministry. It is time to grow up in the area of spiritual gifts and teach others the skills and knowledge the Lord has given you. When you step up to the third level and become the teacher, you will develop your spiritual gifts even further than you imagined possible.

PRAYER

"For this reason I bow my knees to the Father of our Lord Jesus Christ, from whom the whole family in Heaven and Earth is named, that He would grant you, according to the riches of His glory, to be strengthened with might through His Spirit in the inner man, that Christ may dwell in your hearts through faith; that you, being rooted and grounded in love, may be able to comprehend with all the saints what *is* the width and length and depth and height—to know the love of Christ which passes knowledge; that you may be filled with all the fullness of God." (Ephesians 3:14-19)

ADDITIONAL SCRIPTURES FOR FURTHER STUDY

> *"After these things the word of the LORD came to Abram in a vision, saying, 'Do not be afraid, Abram. I am your shield, your exceedingly great reward.'"* (Genesis 15:1)

> *"Then God spoke to Israel in the visions of the night, and said, 'Jacob, Jacob!' And he said, 'Here I am.'"* (Genesis 46:2)

> *"So Samuel lay down until morning, and opened the doors of the house of the LORD. And Samuel*

was afraid to tell Eli the vision." (1 Samuel 3:15)

"According to all these words and according to all this vision, so Nathan spoke to David. (2 Samuel 7:17)

"Now the rest of the acts of Hezekiah, and his goodness, indeed they are written in the vision of Isaiah the prophet, the son of Amoz, and in the book of the kings of Judah and Israel." (2 Chronicles 32:32)

"The vision of Isaiah the son of Amoz, which he saw concerning Judah and Jerusalem in the days of Uzziah, Jotham, Ahaz, and Hezekiah, kings of Judah." (Isaiah 1:1)

"And behold, the glory of the God of Israel was there, like the vision that I saw in the plain." (Ezekiel 8:4)

"Then the Spirit took me up and brought me in a vision by the Spirit of God into Chaldea, to those in captivity. And the vision that I had seen went up from me. So I spoke to those in captivity of all the things the LORD *had shown me."* (Ezekiel 11:24-25)

"Then the secret was revealed to Daniel in a night vision. So Daniel blessed the God of heaven." (Daniel 2:19)

"I have also spoken by the prophets, And have multiplied visions; I have given symbols through the witness of the prophets." (Hosea 12:10)

"The vision of Obadiah. Thus says the Lord GOD concerning Edom (We have heard a report from the LORD, *And a messenger has been sent among the nations, saying, 'Arise, and let us rise up against her for battle')"* (Obadiah 1:1)

"The burden against Nineveh. The book of the vision of Nahum the Elkoshite." (Nahum 1:1)

"Then the LORD *answered me and said: 'Write the vision and make it plain on tablets, that he may run who reads it. For the vision is yet for an appointed time; But at the end it will speak, and it will not lie. Though it tarries, wait for it; Because it will surely come, It will not tarry.'"* (Habakkuk 2:2-3)

"Now as they came down from the mountain, Jesus commanded them, saying, 'Tell the vision to no one until the Son of Man is risen from the dead.'" (Matthew 17:9)

"And the people waited for Zacharias, and marveled that he lingered so long in the temple. But when he came out, he could not speak to them; and they perceived that he had seen a vision in the temple, for he beckoned to them and remained speechless." (Luke 1:21-22)

"Now there was a certain disciple at Damascus named Ananias; and to him the Lord said in a vision, 'Ananias.' And he said, 'Here I am, Lord.' So the Lord said to him, 'Arise and go to the street called Straight, and inquire at the house of Judas for one called Saul of Tarsus, for behold, he is praying. And in a vision he has seen a man named

165

Ananias coming in and putting his hand on him, so that he might receive his sight.'" (Acts 9:10-12)

"About the ninth hour of the day he saw clearly in a vision an angel of God coming in and saying to him, 'Cornelius!'" (Acts 10:3)

"Now while Peter wondered within himself what this vision which he had seen meant, behold, the men who had been sent from Cornelius had made inquiry for Simon's house, and stood before the gate." (Acts 10:17)

"And a vision appeared to Paul in the night. A man of Macedonia stood and pleaded with him, saying, 'Come over to Macedonia and help us.' Now after he had seen the vision, immediately we sought to go to Macedonia, concluding that the Lord had called us to preach the gospel to them." (Acts 16:9-10)

"It is doubtless not profitable for me to boast. I will come to visions and revelations of the Lord: I know a man in Christ who fourteen years ago— whether in the body I do not know, or whether out of the body I do not know, God knows—such a one was caught up to the third heaven." (2 Corinthians 12:1-2)

"And thus I saw the horses in the vision: those who sat on them had breastplates of fiery red, hyacinth blue, and sulfur yellow; and the heads of the horses were like the heads of lions; and out of their mouths came fire, smoke, and brimstone." (Revelation 9:17)

CHAPTER 8

KINGDOM VALUES AND VIRTUES

One morning, I experienced an especially lengthy period of time before being caught up into Heaven. Before I was lifted up into His presence, the Holy Spirit was doing a great deal of work in me. During the Aaronic Blessing, I had asked the Lord to do a special work of renewing my mind to prepare me to serve Him better. I asked the Holy Spirit to fulfill Jesus' promise and guide me into all truth. I asked to know the truth about myself and what I needed to change and what I needed to do to be a better servant of my Lord and my King. He is so faithful, and He took me through the process of dealing with many things in my life. For a short period of time, I thought there might not be a message to send out to my email friends that morning, because so much was being revealed just to me. What I didn't realize at the time was that this was all just the beginning phase of what the Lord was releasing that day.

I began to have visions about areas in the lives of others that needed to be changed. I saw a man miraculously saved from being harmed in an accident. He was angry and embarrassed because he was actually responsible for the accident, but didn't want to admit it. I heard the Lord say, "Great grace was released to him today, but he doesn't know it! He is so easily offended and quick to become angry. He misses so many of the supernatural things I am doing in his life!" I thought about how tragic it is for someone to miss "great grace" coming from the Lord. Then I looked to myself and prayed that I would not make the same mistake.

I saw the Lord speak correction into a woman's spirit through a prophetic word, but she missed it. She reacted with anger against the prophet who brought the message and failed to see that the Lord had sent help to her for the renewing of her mind. I asked the Holy Spirit to help me avoid making this same mistake.

After several of these visions, I was lifted up to a great assembly area in Heaven. What I saw was truly awesome and deeply challenging. I saw a large, circular area made of stones with the Lord sitting on His throne in the center of the circle. Vast armies had assembled before Him. They stood in formation, ready to receive their battle orders. In front of each column, a general stood before the Lord with his helmet off and his head slightly bowed before the Lord. Each of the army formations was shaped like a wedge. There were two behind the general and four behind them and etc. The numbers continued to grow and were beyond counting in the distance behind each general. There were so many that I could not see to the far end of each formation. I could see that these armies were made up of both saints and angels from the hosts of Heaven.

I then counted and took notice of the fact that there were seven generals at the head of seven armies assembled before the Lord. I understood that seven spoke of the fullness of all those who will stand with the Lord in the great and final battle of human history. Then my spiritual eyes were opened further and I could see that one of the Seven Spirits of God was standing at the head of each army. The Holy Spirit stood between the generals and Jesus in each formation. The Seven Spirits were very close to the Lord and literally surrounded Him with their presence. There was a spirit of expectancy and excitement in the air around the throne of Jesus which spread out to the entire host assembled before Him. Everyone seemed to feel ready for what was ahead. However, it was quickly revealed that they were not as ready as they had assumed. Beginning with each general, the Lord was revealing areas in them which were still not in full submission to His authority.

I suddenly realized why I had to go through so much correction that morning. My time of correction was preparing me to understand what each of them was experiencing. I could not look at them with judgment and condemnation. I was in the same situation they were in. We are all in need of correction in order to prepare us for the great end time harvest and for the battle at the end of the age. We all have blind spots which block us from seeing our own faults. We quickly see the areas which need to change in others while failing to see our own. I remembered what Jesus said:

> *"Judge not, that you be not judged. For with what judgment you judge, you will be judged; and with the measure you use, it will be measured back to you. And why do you look at the speck in your brother's eye, but do not consider the plank in your own eye? Or how can you say to your brother, 'Let me remove the speck from your eye'; and look, a plank is in your own eye? Hypocrite! First remove the plank from your own eye, and then you will see clearly to remove the speck from your brother's eye."* (Matthew 7:1-5)

My time with the Lord began with a log removing experience. My own eye needed to be cleared before I could even think about the speck in someone else's eye. Until the healing of my own eyes was completed, I was in no place to deal with someone else. I was not even allowed to see the specks in others until my own spiritual eyes were opened to see what the Lord was removing and releasing that day.

There is an anointing for removing logs from our eyes. This does not mean that the Lord is anointing us to judge others.

This is a log removing season provided so that the Lord can prepare us for something powerful which will soon manifest. This is our time to get prepared so that we can participate. All of the generals had enough humility to be willing to accept correction and discipline. This is one of the reasons they have been placed in such positions of authority. We cannot lead others if we are not willing to be led by the Lord. We cannot help deliver others from the works of the devil unless we are ready for more deliverance in our lives.

Then the Lord reminded me of one more very important teaching which he released in the twentieth chapter of the book of Matthew:

> *"Jesus called them together and said, 'You know that the rulers of the Gentiles lord it over them, and their high officials exercise authority over them. Not so with you. Instead, whoever wants to become great among you must be your servant, and whoever wants to be first must be your slave—just as the Son of Man did not come to be served, but to serve, and to give his life as a ransom for many.'"* (Matthew 20:25-28, NIV)

May we have ears to hear and eyes to see what the Lord is saying and doing in our lives today and every day. Amen!

CHARACTER IS IMPORTANT!
(Especially in the kingdom of God)

> *"Who may ascend into the hill of the LORD? Or who may stand in His holy place? He who has clean hands and a pure heart, who has not lifted up his soul to an idol, nor sworn deceitfully. He shall receive blessing from the LORD, and righteousness from the God of his salvation. This is*

Jacob, the generation of those who seek Him, who seek Your face." (Psalm 24:3-6)

I do not see very much training these days which focuses on the development of character. Some people seem very fatalistic about it and simply shrug it off, saying, "You either have it or you don't!" However, genetics cannot account for the presence or absence of character. It cannot be inherited from your parents. It must be learned by each individual in each and every generation. The lessons which build character are not easy and some people choose to avoid the difficult things in life. I remember what Paul taught about the development of character:

"Therefore, having been justified by faith, we have peace with God through our Lord Jesus Christ, through whom also we have access by faith into this grace in which we stand, and rejoice in hope of the glory of God. And not only that, but we also glory in tribulations, knowing that tribulation produces perseverance; and perseverance, character; and character, hope. Now hope does not disappoint, because the love of God has been poured out in our hearts by the Holy Spirit who was given to us." (Romans 5:1-5)

It is that tribulation part which most of us would like to avoid. However, tribulation is the crucible in which character begins to emerge. Without it, there simply is no further development or learning. Unfortunately, we can only learn small lessons through the experiences of others. We learn them more fully and value them more highly when our learning comes from our own painful experiences. Paul is saying that without tribulation, we never really develop the important characteristic of perseverance. It is in the very act of persevering through hardships that true character begins to emerge. The good news is that our Christian hope then comes forward to assure us of the love of God and the gifts of the Holy Spirit.

We like to judge others by their character more than we appreciate being judged by ours. Paul told the Philippian Church that they could trust Timothy as a minister because his character had already been proven to them in the past.

> *"But I trust in the Lord Jesus to send Timothy to you shortly, that I also may be encouraged when I know your state. For I have no one like-minded, who will sincerely care for your state. For all seek their own, not the things which are of Christ Jesus. But you know his proven character, that as a son with his father he served with me in the gospel."* (Philippians 2:19-22)

We appreciate the comfort and confidence which comes from knowing that those who minister to us and among us have proven character. Are we equally willing for our character to be proven to others? This is the challenging question for all disciples of Jesus Christ.

Some people have challenged me on this view, claiming that I am trying to bring back a form of legalism to the church. They say that people don't receive salvation through their works, so we should avoid all emphasis on works, which are the proof of character. This challenge represents a serious misunderstanding of scripture and especially Paul's teachings. He repeatedly pointed to the need to develop character and for churches to choose leaders of proven character. One example is found in His letter to a young minister named Titus.

> *"For this reason I left you in Crete, that you should set in order the things that are lacking, and appoint elders in every city as I commanded you—if a man is blameless, the husband of*

one wife, having faithful children not accused of dissipation or insubordination. For a bishop must be blameless, as a steward of God, not self-willed, not quick-tempered, not given to wine, not violent, not greedy for money, but hospitable, a lover of what is good, sober-minded, just, holy, self-controlled, holding fast the faithful word as he has been taught, that he may be able, by sound doctrine, both to exhort and convict those who contradict. For there are many insubordinate, both idle talkers and deceivers, especially those of the circumcision, whose mouths must be stopped, who subvert whole households, teaching things which they ought not, for the sake of dishonest gain." (Titus 1:5-11)

Paul gave similar instructions to Timothy. These passages focus attention on people who would be leaders in the church. I would like to expand that to all believers. Our witness to the world is damaged every time someone in the body of Christ comes to light revealing a serious lack of character. The enemy wants to wave all our failures in front of the world in order to discredit the faith and bring shame on the church. As we work to build character, we are denying Him this opportunity to do his primary work as the "accuser."

Another reason to build character is actually of a much greater importance than public opinion or selecting people for leadership. It has to do with desiring to please the Lord. When we are born again, we develop a desire to build character in order to please God. It is not about legalism. It is about trying to be the man or woman our wonderful Father God created us to be. One of the most powerful statements of love I have heard was from a man who wanted to be a better person for his spouse and his children. When you truly love someone, you desire to be a better person for them. What is true in our physical relationships is even more true in our spiritual relationship with the Father, Jesus, and the Holy Spirit. Becoming who God wants us to be is a process. It is not an end state during this lifetime. We must daily seek to be transformed into His likeness.

> *"And do not be conformed to this world, but be transformed by the renewing of your mind, that you may prove what is that good and acceptable and perfect will of God."* (Romans 12:2)

If you want to please God, it is important to be intentional about who you have as friends and associates. We tend to become like the people we associate with on a regular basis. If you spend time with people who are blatantly wicked and perverse, it affects your character. Before long, you will hear yourself saying the things they say. You will find yourself doing the same things they do. It is always a good idea to associate with people you admire and then strive to be more like them. Remember what Paul said to the Corinthian Church:

> *"Do not be misled: Bad company corrupts good character."* (1 Corinthians 15:33, NIV)

If you spend time with people who have noble character and truly love the Lord, you will tend to become more and more like them. You will find yourself saying the righteous things they say. You will also find yourself doing the noble things they are doing. If that works out well for you, then take it up another notch. Think about this: in like manner, if you spend time with God, you become more like Him. This is one of the reasons for us to spend more time walking and talking with the Lord. His character rubs off on ours. We begin to like and love what He values. We begin to do something Jesus always did: we say what we hear Him saying. We will find ourselves trying to do what we see Him doing. This is one of the most powerful ways to grow character, and it feels much better than going through the pain of tribulation.

It is important for us to consciously decide to develop character. It doesn't happen by accident. We would all like to be able to just pray for it and receive it. Praying for it and seeking it passionately is one of the ways to receive from the Father. However, to really make it ours, we must still go through the learning process.

I believe that everyone admires someone of strong character.

> *"A wife of noble character who can find? She is worth far more than rubies."* (Proverbs 31:10, NIV)

We value people who are strong, stable, and reliable. It is much easier to become close to people we can trust. To stay close, we must become that kind of person for our families, our friends, our co-workers, and our God.

CHARACTER IS CRITICAL TO LIVING UNDER AN OPEN HEAVEN

Character has a side benefit—it brings favor. It brings favor from God.

> *"And now, my daughter, don't be afraid. I will do for you all you ask. All my fellow townsmen know that you are a woman of noble character."* (Ruth 3:11, NIV)

The story of Ruth and Boaz is a lesson which is clearly related to the relationship between the Lord and His bride. We like the part of Ruth's story about her being swept off her feet, brought out of poverty and lack into wealth and comfort, and being included in the lineage of Jesus Christ. What we can easily miss is that the focus of this passage is on the noble character of Ruth. Boaz responded positively to Ruth because he had seen her character and knew that she was trustworthy. Ruth's noble character didn't just happen. It was developed during a time of great difficulty, pain, and loss. Her persistence and endurance after losing her husband, living through a time of famine, and leaving her family to go to another country with her mother-in-law were all part of the price she paid to develop these personality traits. It was these character traits which attracted Boaz to Ruth and opened the door for her to become his bride.

People have asked me; "Where is the 'unconditional love' of God in this story which would cause Him to allow her to go through all this tribulation?" I ask them to show me in the Bible any reference to the "unconditional love" of God. It is not a Biblical teaching. From Genesis to Revelation, the message is unchanged. The favor of God and the blessings which flow from that favor are conditional on obedience. Obedience and persistence during times of hardship produce character. God responds to noble character by releasing His favor. Some argue that this all changed with Jesus. They try to attribute unconditional love to Jesus. I recommend that you read Jesus' teaching again. He is consistent. His love, blessings, and favor are all conditional. They come out of our love for and obedience to Him.

> *"Jesus replied, 'If anyone loves me, he will obey my teaching. My Father will love him, and we will come to him and make our home with him. He who does not love me will not obey my teaching. These words you hear are not my own; they belong to the Father who sent me.'"* (John 14:23-24, NIV)

> *"As the Father has loved me, so have I loved*

you. Now remain in my love. If you obey my com-
mands, you will remain in my love, just as I have
obeyed my Father's commands and remain in his
love. I have told you this so that my joy may be in
you and that your joy may be complete." (John
15:9-11, NIV)

Jesus did not take the disciples out of the world, but allowed them to go through tribulation to develop their character and make them more fit for greater service. In order to please God and be welcome in His presence, build on your character. Ask for His help. Rely on the Holy Spirit to guide you in the process. Remember: to accomplish His purpose in your life, you must develop strong character.

"Keep a firm grasp on both your character and
your teaching. Don't be diverted. Just keep at it.
Both you and those who hear you will experience
salvation." (1 Timothy 4:16, TMSG)

I hope I have been very clear about one thing: Character comes at a cost. Remember Paul's teaching to the church in Rome:

"And not only that, but we also glory in tribu-
lations, knowing that tribulation produces per-
severance; and perseverance, character; and
character, hope." (Romans 5:3-4)

When we are first introduced to Jacob in the Bible, it is clear that he had a character defect. Even his name indicated the nature of the defect. The name *Jacob* means "one who sup-plants," or "the crooked one." Jacob manipulated his brother and his father to get a birthright and a blessing which were not his. In fear of his brother's wrath, he had to flee to another land.

During all the hardship and difficulty of his time in Laban's hire, Jacob learned character. He had to work 14 years to have Rachel for his wife. He was promised that he would only have to work seven years, but got a dose of his own medicine from his uncle, Laban. He had to overcome his disappointment and endure hardship and danger to develop the character he would need to become what God had called him to be. It was only after he learned these lessons that the Lord changed his name and released his destiny.

"And He said, 'Your name shall no longer be called Jacob, but Israel; for you have struggled with God and with men, and have prevailed.'" (Genesis 32:28)

Jacob's new name meant "Prince of God." What a shift! He went from being the "one who supplants" to being the Prince of God. What an elevation in kingdom authority! After his struggles and hardships, Jacob knew how to value his relationship with God and understand his calling. If you value your relationship with God, you will work for it. If you desire Him and that kind of relationship with your whole heart, you will get to the task now.

"So don't lose a minute in building on what you've been given, complementing your basic faith with good character, spiritual understanding, alert discipline, passionate patience, reverent wonder, warm friendliness, and generous love, each dimension fitting into and developing the others. With these qualities active and growing in your lives, no grass will grow under your feet, no day will pass without its reward as you mature in your experience of our Master Jesus. Without these qualities you can't see what's right

before you, oblivious that your old sinful life has been wiped off the books. So, friends, confirm God's invitation to you, his choice of you. Don't put it off; do it now. Do this, and you'll have your life on a firm footing, the streets paved and the way wide open into the eternal kingdom of our Master and Savior, Jesus Christ." (2 Peter 1:5-11, TMSG)

TO UNDERSTAND WHO GOD IS, STUDY HIS CHARACTER

If you want to know God better, learn what He values. If you want to walk more closely with Him, learn to value what He values. If you want to visit in the Third Heaven, develop the type of character which is always welcome in Heaven. We have a great teacher who also modeled God's character.

"I spelled out your character in detail to the men and women you gave me. They were yours in the first place; Then you gave them to me, And they have now done what you said." (John 17:6, TMSG)

If we want to spend time with Him in Heaven, we need to be ready to let go of everything which displeases Him.

"Since, then, we do not have the excuse of ignorance, everything—and I do mean everything—connected with that old way of life has to go. It's rotten through and through. Get rid of it! And then take on an entirely new way of life—a God-fashioned life, a life renewed from the inside and working itself into your conduct as God accu-

179

rately reproduces his character in you." (Ephesians 4:22-24, TMSG)

I like the way this passage is translated in The Message Bible. It spells out very clearly a promise from God. The promise in this passage is that God will accurately reproduce His character in us. Human teachers may give a good description of God's character and help to train you to be more like Him. But only the Lord can and will "accurately reproduce His character in you." I like that! I want that! I seek that! I am going to press in more and more to receive this promise. I value visiting with Him in Heaven beyond what I can describe for you. It is my passion and my highest desire to be able to visit with Him in this personal way every day. I am committed to doing everything I can to maintain the opening into Heaven for these visits. How about you?

SEEK TO KNOW AND APPROPRIATE
THE VALUES OF GOD

"Grace and peace be multiplied to you in the knowledge of God and of Jesus our Lord, as His divine power has given to us all things that pertain to life and godliness, through the knowledge of Him who called us by glory and virtue, by which have been given to us exceedingly great and precious promises, that through these you may be partakers of the divine nature, having escaped the corruption that is in the world through lust." (2 Peter 1:2-4)

It is possible to know what God values. He has revealed Himself in several ways. When we see Jesus, we have seen the Father. The better we know Jesus and the more time we spend with Him as we obediently follow, the better we will know the character and values of Father God. He has given us the written

Word and so much of His character is revealed in our Bibles. However, you have to read it and make it a special study to learn about His characteristics in order to get the full benefit. Did you know that more than 65% of the people who label themselves "born again Christians" seldom or never read the Bible? Of those who do read the Bible, did you know that the majority only read it during church or organized group Bible studies? Many others only look at it when they are in deep trouble, and then they don't know how to find what they are looking for. There is a real shortage of Bible-believing people who know what the Bible says. Yet, this is where we go to learn the characteristics and values of God the Father.

The third great source of information about the character of God is the Holy Spirit. It is one of His primary purposes to lead us in developing an understanding of the Lord. I want you to know with certainty that God is a loving Father and He is not withholding the things you need. He is the giver of the gifts which produce His fruit.

> *"But the fruit of the Spirit is love, joy, peace, longsuffering, kindness, goodness, faithfulness, gentleness, self-control. Against such there is no law. And those who are Christ's have crucified the flesh with its passions and desires. If we live in the Spirit, let us also walk in the Spirit."* (Galatians 5:22-24)

> *"Do not be deceived, my beloved brethren. Every good gift and every perfect gift is from above, and comes down from the Father of lights, with whom there is no variation or shadow of turning. Of His own will He brought us forth by the word of truth, that we might be a kind of firstfruits of His creatures."* (James 1:16-18)

So what are the character traits which God values in us? They are the same character traits which He demonstrates toward us. The very same traits God reveals to us about Himself are the character traits He values in us. There is no mystery here. He has revealed it all through Jesus, His Word, and the Holy Spirit. Study to understand the lesson Paul was trying to teach the Corinthian church in the passage below:

> *"We give no offense in anything, that our ministry may not be blamed. But in all things we commend ourselves as ministers of God: in much patience, in tribulations, in needs, in distresses, in stripes, in imprisonments, in tumults, in labors, in sleeplessness, in fastings; by purity, by knowledge, by longsuffering, by kindness, by the Holy Spirit, by sincere love, by the word of truth, by the power of God, by the armor of righteousness on the right hand and on the left, by honor and dishonor, by evil report and good report; as deceivers, and yet true; as unknown, and yet well known; as dying, and behold we live; as chastened, and yet not killed; as sorrowful, yet always rejoicing; as poor, yet making many rich; as having nothing, and yet possessing all things."* (2 Corinthians 6:3-10)

WE ARE COMMANDED TO BECOME IMITATORS OF GOD

> *"Therefore be imitators of God as dear children. And walk in love, as Christ also has loved us and given Himself for us, an offering and a sacrifice to God for a sweet-smelling aroma."* (Ephesians 5:1-2)

It is very significant that Paul focuses on love to explain how we are to be imitators of God. Jesus walked in this kind of love and could boldly proclaim that if we have seen Him, we have seen the Father. If we are to imitate God and imitate Christ Jesus, our main focus has to be on loving as He has loved us.

> *"And we have known and believed the love that God has for us. God is love, and he who abides in love abides in God, and God in him."* (1 John 4:16)

It is not really possible to live in love unless you live in Him. Human love, at its best, is a pale shadow of the true love of God. Jesus exhibited this fullness of God's love while in deep agony on the cross. He prayed for those who persecuted and condemned Him to death. He sincerely asked Father God to forgive them. In His passionate love for them, He recognized that they didn't really understand what they were doing. It is extremely rare for human beings to love those who are seeking to damage them. It is even more rare for someone to love another person who is intentionally hurting them and seeking their death. This is a God-kind of love that we cannot fully attain in this lifetime. But we continue to try. We make it our goal and our purpose. If you want to be with Him in the Third Heaven, it is important to be constantly striving to imitate Him and to imitate His redeeming love.

> *"Therefore, as God's chosen people, holy and dearly loved, clothe yourselves with compassion, kindness, humility, gentleness and patience. Bear with each other and forgive whatever grievances you may have against one another. Forgive as the Lord forgave you. And over all these virtues put on love, which binds them all together in perfect unity."* (Colossians 3:12-14, NIV)

I like the imagery of putting these God-like characteristics on like clothing. We aspire to be what the Lord wants us to be, but sometimes the changes are slow in coming. But, in the meantime, we wear God's characteristics like our outer garments. We are not putting on an act. We are putting His nature on over ours. We are sincerely working to attain it and in the meantime we want to serve Him as if it has already manifested.

This is a matter of the heart and what your heart desires is extremely important. It is your heart which needs to change and not your clothing. This only happens as your heart is changed by His love and through His promise and commitment to "accurately reproduce his character in you." (Ephesians 4:24, TMSG)

> *"So rend your heart, and not your garments; Return to the LORD your God, For He is gracious and merciful, slow to anger, and of great kindness; and He relents from doing harm."* (Joel 2:13)

Rending your heart sounds painful. Most real and lasting changes do involve pain. Growing involves pain. If we want to grow up into the image of the Lord, we must necessarily go through these challenging processes. Paul gives us some good advice about how to keep the right thoughts in our minds while we are being transformed.

> *"Finally, brethren, whatever things are true, whatever things are noble, whatever things are just, whatever things are pure, whatever things are lovely, whatever things are of good report, if there is any virtue and if there is anything praiseworthy—meditate on these things. The things which you learned and received and heard and saw in me, these do, and the God of peace will be with you."* (Philippians 4:8-9)

I have turned to this passage many times as life has presented great challenges to me. When you are tempted to think the worst of others, go back to this word, and make the shift to God's kind of thinking. When you have been hurt by others and the thoughts and memories keep coming back to you, turn to this passage and begin to identify actual ways in which God has given these good things to you. What are the truly pure things He has brought into your life? Can you recall some truly beautiful experiences the Lord has provided for you in the past? Think on these things. Have you seen people whose behavior warrants a good report? Have you witnessed true virtue in another person? Can you think of something praiseworthy about a fellow believer? After meditating on these things, try to go deeper. Can you remember when the person who seems to have hurt you has manifested these same good characteristics? If you can honestly do that—remember those things rather than the things which have offended you – then you are truly being an imitator of God.

There is really no excuse for being unaware of God's awesome character. He has manifested it in so many ways. Sometimes I just go out and look at a sunset or a starry sky and meditate on my awesome creator, Father God. It truly changes my perspective.

> *"For since the creation of the world His invisible attributes are clearly seen, being understood by the things that are made, even His eternal power and Godhead, so that they are without excuse, because, although they knew God, they did not glorify Him as God, nor were thankful, but became futile in their thoughts, and their foolish hearts were darkened. Professing to be wise, they became fools, and changed the glory of the incorruptible God into an image made like corruptible man— and birds and four-footed animals and creeping things.* (Romans 1:20-23)

PRAYER

"And this is my prayer: that your love may abound more and more in knowledge and depth of insight, so that you may be able to discern what is best and may be pure and blameless until the day of Christ, filled with the fruit of righteousness that comes through Jesus Christ—to the glory and praise of God." (Philippians 1:9-11, NIV)

On the next page is an exercise to assist you in identifying God's character. Go through the list and make a check mark by those things you already imitate and put an "x" after those things which you desire to imitate in the future. As you grow and develop His character, go back over the list and note things which have changed. Celebrate every area of growth as you give the Lord the praise and glory for every positive outcome in your life and ministry.

CHARACTER EXERCISE

GOD IS:	I AM:	I WANT TO BE
Love		
Light		
Creative		
Kind hearted		
Good		
One		
Gracious		
Faithful		
Wise		
Spirit		
True		
Patient		
Righteous		
Just		
Salvation		
Merciful		
Holy		
Strong		
Long suffering		
A man of war		

CHAPTER 9

TURNING UP THE VOLUME

As I went face down before the Lord, I was carried in the Spirit to a place in Heaven which I had not seen before. An older woman was standing in front of me talking, but I couldn't hear any sound. I looked at her for a short while, and then moved on. However, she was in front of me again. This time she was seated on a chair that was fairly high up. Again, she was speaking, but I couldn't hear any sound. She was very persistent and seemed to think that she was saying something I was supposed to hear. I continued to look at her, but could not hear any sound. Then I was taken in the Spirit to another place which I did recognize.

As soon as I left the place where the woman was located, I heard the Lord say, "You said you wanted to meet her." In my mind I wondered who she was. Then the Lord said, "She is Maria Woodworth-Etter, and you have been saying how wonderful it would have been to meet her and hear her preaching." I had just completed reading her biography and had said that several times, but I had not expected to meet her like this. Wow! I missed an awesome opportunity.

Then the Lord directed my attention to a high fence made of metal. It looked like one of those wrought iron fences in front of a mansion. I had dreamed several times in the last couple of weeks that I was putting bronze plates on this fence. The bronze plates had the names of people whose mission on Earth was complete and arrows pointed in the direction they were to go to enter their reward. The bronze plate on the left had an arrow pointing to the right and the plate on the right had an arrow pointing to the left. Each person was being directed to something special designed just for them, and it was in a direction other than what was expected. Their rewards were to be greater than they had asked or imagined. I couldn't remember the names I had seen on these signs in the dreams, and now I couldn't read the names. This all seemed kind of odd and a little frustrating.

I was then carried in the Spirit to a third place where I stood before the Lord. The Lord said, "The key to carrying a mantle previously worn by another is to honor the ones who have gone before. You were in such a rush to get to a place where you could receive what you were seeking that you missed what I was giving to you."

I had been seeking the word from Heaven for that day and was focused on getting to a place where I could receive it. The woman had seemed like a distraction. I knew in my spirit that there was something special about her, but I didn't ask or pause to find out what she meant to me. Since I could not hear what she was saying, I made a poor assumption that the message was not for me. I pray that I will have another opportunity to meet this woman who did such an awesome work for the Lord under such great adversity. I wanted to go back and wait to meet the people being directed by the words on the bronze plates, but it didn't happen. Then I began to understand that the message from Heaven was not about what these people had to say, but to help us understand what the Lord is saying.

In this season, mantles are being released which have been worn by others before us. In our rush to get what we want or to press in for more, we have not always taken the time to honor those who have gone before us. Which of God's generals wore a mantle you would like to wear? Have you taken time to honor them? Have you taken time to gain an understanding of the price they paid for carrying that mantle? Have you considered that you will have to pay the same price to wear it in your generation? Knowing you will pay the price should raise your level of value for that forefather or mother who endured so much to pass it down to you.

Then I understood that this is part of the humility we must walk in if we want to carry the mantle. Human pride will disqualify us so quickly. When we look to those who have gone before and see the magnitude of what the Lord worked through them, it is truly a humbling experience. Are you ready to receive the mantle the Lord is giving in this season? Are you ready to carry the fire of revival to this generation? Are you ready to pay the price?

Begin even now to understand and honor those who have gone before you. We are standing on the shoulders of giants. When we reach a higher level, it is often because of them and not because of something we have done. When something awesome comes through our ministry, it is only because of what the Lord is doing. Remember what Jesus said:

> *"I am the vine; you are the branches. If a man remains in me and I in him, he will bear much fruit; apart from me you can do nothing."* (John 15:5, NIV)

And, remember what Paul said to the church at Philippi:

> *"I can do all things through Christ who strengthens me."* (Philippians 4:13)

Knowing this, where is the place for human pride? May we learn to honor our fathers and mothers (natural and spiritual parents) so that the Lord can work through us as He did them.

TURNING UP THE VOLUME

After the Lord gave this title to me along with an outline for this chapter, I discovered that this section of the book was the most challenging for me. I delayed working on this one longer than the others. There were several reasons for this hesitancy which I didn't initially understand.

Turning up the volume in terms of sound is necessary and painful for me. I spent almost 30 years on active duty as an Army Chaplain and over five and a half years in the Army Reserves as an artillery officer. My ears paid a price for this service. I have received healing from the Lord and I try to protect my hearing from further damage. So I am sensitive to the volume of sound coming to my ears.

The second difficulty I faced was in understanding what the title really meant. It took time and prayer for me to understand that the message is about more than sound. The word "volume" has several meanings. In addition to sound levels, it can mean the amount of space an object occupies. It can refer to pages put together in a book or one book in a series. It can be a measure of the flow of liquid substances. Learning this didn't make the task easier, but expanded the possibilities exponentially.

Each time the Lord led me to work on a particular chapter of this book, He released a vision to increase the fullness (volume) of the chapter. My third challenge was waiting for a vision to go with this chapter. Finally, the Lord revealed to me that He had already released the vision. I had to go back several months to find the vision which you saw at the beginning of this chapter. The difficulty was not from the Lord, but from my own resistance. I realized that I needed to increase the volume in my spirit to more clearly hear what the Lord is revealing. Sometimes the Lord's voice seems so soft and subtle. I remembered how the Lord sounded to Elijah following the wind, earthquake and fire.

> *"Then He [God] said, 'Go out, and stand on the mountain before the Lord.' And behold, the Lord passed by, and a great and strong wind tore into the mountains and broke the rocks in pieces before the Lord, but the Lord was not in the wind; and after the wind an earthquake, but the Lord was not in the earthquake; and after the earthquake a fire, but the Lord was not in the fire; and after the fire <u>a still small voice</u>."* (1 Kings 19:11-12)

Elijah's response to hearing the voice is instructive. He first wrapped his face in his mantle. He wanted to hide himself from the presence of the Lord. He had been overwhelmed by fear and ran from the threats of Jezebel. Hiding out in the cave didn't leave him feeling worthy of the presence of the Lord. So he tried to cover himself. He also wanted to hide from the truth. His despair had left him unable to recover his spiritual authority and get back in the spiritual battle with King Ahab and Jezebel. I believe he knew what was coming next.

> *"So it was, when Elijah heard it, that he wrapped his face in his mantle and went out and stood in the entrance of the cave. Suddenly a voice came to him, and said, 'What are you doing here, Elijah?'"* (1 Kings 19:13)

The Lord told him to go back and anoint his replacement. When we cover our ears to avoid the truth, it is difficult to hear what the Lord is saying. We need to open up and listen to what the Lord is trying to say to us. We need to turn up the volume rather than attempting to tune Him out.

In the Lord's revelation to Ezekiel, He pointed out another problem which hinders our ability to hear in the spirit. The spirit of rebellion will block your ability to hear.

*"Now the word of the LORD came to me, saying:
'Son of man, you dwell in the midst of a rebellious house, which has eyes to see but does not
see, and ears to hear but does not hear; for they
are a rebellious house.'"* (Ezekiel 12:1-2)

We need to repent of any rebellion in our own spiritual walk in order to hear more clearly. This is a turning up of the volume. After we deal with this spirit in our own lives, we have to deal with it among our people (the body of Christ). The spirit of rebellion has been running rampant in the church during the last few years. Perhaps it has been rampant throughout human history. We cannot simply ignore it and expect the Lord to do something. He places the task back on us.

This theme of having ears to hear but not hearing recurs over and over in scripture. In the New Testament, Jesus speaks of this phenomenon in Matthew 11:15, Matthew 13:9, Matthew 13:43, Mark 4:9, Mark 4:23, Mark 7:16, Luke 8:8, and Luke 14:35. These scriptures are referring to God's people (not unbelievers) failing to use their ears for hearing His word. All of these passages are making a reference to the reality that this is a matter of choice. People who have been born with ears to hear have decided not to hear the Lord because they have a rebellious spirit. It may take a greater miracle to heal ears intentionally closed than natural ears which were never fully developed in the mother's womb. It may be more of a miracle to open the ears of a rebellious person than ears which have been severely damaged.

Many people try to blame their shortfalls on the Lord. They claim that the problem is on His part because He isn't speaking to them or that He is not speaking loud enough for them to hear. As the title of this chapter implies, we have the volume control. If we want to hear more clearly, we need to turn up the volume. Remember: all you have to do is ask. Consider the two passages below:

"If you then, being evil, know how to give good gifts to your children, how much more will your Father who is in heaven give good things to those who ask Him!" (Matthew 7:11)

"If you then, being evil, know how to give good gifts to your children, how much more will your heavenly Father give the Holy Spirit to those who ask Him!" (Luke 11:13)

The Lord is not the source of our problem. For some people, it may be because they lack the spiritual gift to hear. All they need to do is ask and they will receive it. For others, it may be because they are listening to the flesh rather than the Spirit. All they need to do is repent and ask the Lord to get them back to the position of following the leadership of the Holy Spirit.

Here is something to consider: God is speaking! He is speaking whether we choose to listen or not. Think for a few minutes about what the Bible says about God speaking. In the beginning, God spoke everything into being. He walked and talked with Adam and Eve in the garden. He has been speaking to His prophets, people, and anointed leaders ever since the fall in the garden.

One of the greatest tragedies in human history is that His people do not choose to listen. Every great human tragedy and every moral and spiritual decline begins with people refusing to listen to the Lord.

"Now Moses called all Israel and said to them: 'You have seen all that the LORD did before your eyes in the land of Egypt, to Pharaoh and to all his servants and to all his land—the great trials which your eyes have seen, the signs, and those great wonders. Yet the LORD has not given you a heart to perceive and eyes to see and ears to hear, to this very day.'" (Deuteronomy 29:2-4)

Notice, first of all, that Moses was not saying that it is God's fault. He was saying that, although God has been speaking, He does not force people to listen to His voice. The Lord continued (and He continues) to speak to those who are willing to listen. What kind of person are you? Are you ready and willing to listen to the Lord? Remember that one of the reasons the Lord doesn't let some people visit the Third Heaven is His grace. If He tells you something He wants you to do while you are in Heaven and you choose not to obey, judgment comes quickly. Thus, the Lord is not putting people into a position of danger where they may be in line for His wrath. He wants what is best for you and is working to provide what you need and want at the right time. He waits until He knows that you are ready to obey. If you have been waiting for a long time, you might want to get with Him and receive His help in dealing with a spirit of rebellion.

I discovered another truth as I was praying and thinking through the writing of this chapter. There are people who do not hear and have made the wrong choice, but instead of seeking the Lord's help to hear, they begin to teach that God does not speak to people any longer. They seem to believe that this is an acceptable excuse. They are proposing that if God isn't speaking, they have no obligation to be listening. This is contrary to scripture and to my experience. Instead of following the doctrines of man, we need faith to believe that He speaks and we can hear. Remember what Paul taught in the fourteenth chapter of Corinthians:

> *"Pursue love, and desire spiritual gifts, but especially that you may prophesy."* (1 Corinthians 14:1)

Again, notice the order of things in this passage. First of all, pursue love. Pursue your love for the Lord by listening to His Word and trusting Him to provide what He promises. He is the keeper of His Word! Next, pursue the gift of love to love others as the Lord has loved you. Then, and only then, earnestly desire spiritual gifts (especially spiritual hearing). It is okay to want all of the spiritual gifts, and it is okay to ask for all of them. Some people quote the passage below as an excuse:

> *"for to one is given the word of wisdom through the Spirit, to another the word of knowledge through the same Spirit."* (1 Corinthians 12:8)

Using this verse (or misusing this verse), they claim that we only get one gift each and that we should not ask for more. The same person who wrote this passage wrote 1 Corinthians 14:1 in which we are commanded to desire gifts (more than one). You can trust the Holy Spirit. He will not give you more than God wills for you. He will not give you gifts you are unable to handle. He will only give you the gifts which match the level of your love. So continue to pursue love.

Finally, Paul commands you to go after the gift of prophesy more than the other gifts. If you earnestly desire spiritual gifts, how can you lift one higher than the others? This is something of a mystery at first. As I sought revelation about this, I came to understand that, as I pursue prophesy with special intensity, it does not take away from my desire for other gifts. On the contrary, it elevates the desire and each desire goes higher and higher. I want to be one who pursues, overtakes and restores all the gifts to the church. How about you?

Notice that when Jesus said over and over, "He who has ears to hear, let him hear," He was speaking to people who have physical ears. It is also clear that they have spiritual ears. So, what's the problem? Obviously, these people have made a decision not to hear. They have chosen to waste one of God's very precious gifts. This is truly tragic. God created us with these wonderful, natural gifts and then released spiritual gifts through the work of the Holy Spirit. But these facts do not outweigh another fact.

God created us with free will and He honors our choices. The Lord always invites and encourages us to make better choices (i.e. choose life)

> *"I call heaven and earth as witnesses today against you, that I have set before you life and death, blessing and cursing; therefore choose life, that both you and your descendants may live; that you may love the LORD your God, that you may obey His voice, and that you may cling to Him, for He is your life and the length of your days; and that you may dwell in the land which the LORD swore to your fathers, to Abraham, Isaac, and Jacob, to give them."* (Deuteronomy 30:19-20)

Did you notice that in this passage, the choice for life results in being able to hear and obey His voice? This statement is not accidental and should not be taken lightly. This is the revelation of a powerful spiritual key. Choose life and, in so doing, you are also choosing to hear the voice of the Lord!

Tragically, some would rather hear what the world is saying. They prefer to hear about the pleasures and opportunities of the flesh. They foolishly choose short-term pleasure over eternal joy. Their focus on the natural is so strong that it blocks out the things of the spirit. You can get so caught up in the flesh that you become hearing impaired. If you have done this, you need to learn how to turn up the volume on the Lord's voice which is constantly speaking to your spirit. More correctly, you need to turn up the volume on your hearing devices (natural and spiritual).

One of the passages of scripture which causes me to tremble for some is in Hebrews 6.

> *"For it is impossible for those who were once enlightened, and have tasted the heavenly gift, and have become partakers of the Holy Spirit,*

*and have tasted the good word of God and the
powers of the age to come, if they fall away, to
renew them again to repentance, since they cru-
cify again for themselves the Son of God, and put
Him to an open shame."* (Hebrews 6:4-6)

One thing I know for sure: I never want to be in this place in
my relationship with the Lord. And I do not want to see anyone
else in this spiritual condition. Wow! This is just very hard to
comprehend. Some people choose not to believe it. But another
thing I know is that you cannot pick and choose the parts of the
Bible you want to believe right now. It is all or nothing. You
either believe it or you do not believe it. Consider this passage
as you pray for the lost and for those who are close to falling
away. Pray for those who are making poor choices. We hearken
back to the message Moses had to give:

*"I call heaven and earth as witnesses today
against you, that I have set before you life and
death, blessing and cursing; therefore choose
life, that both you and your descendants may
live; that you may love the Lord your God, that
you may obey His voice, and that you may cling
to Him, for He is your life and the length of your
days."* (Deuteronomy 30:19-20a)

People who choose not to hear the voice of the Lord have
turned up the volume of the world to block out God's voice. I
heard about a man who noticed a strange noise from his car and
took it in for diagnosis and repair. The repairman was unable to
find any mechanical problem with the car and diagnosed this
as a radio problem. When the man asked what that meant, the
mechanic replied, "Turn up the volume on your radio until you
can't hear the noise anymore."

The noise from the car was blocked, but the problem still

existed. That's exactly what happens when we turn up the volume of the flesh to block God's voice. One thing I have come to believe is that our need to "hear Him and live" is not diminished by the noise of the world. Simply turning up the volume of the flesh will not excuse you from God's calling. It will never be an acceptable excuse when we face Him at the seat of judgment. It is much better to work it out now so that you can live in the fullness of the blessing now and experience the joy of His presence every day. I have found that this produces much better fruit in my life and fruit for eternal life. And better still, there are no bad side effects.

TIME TO HEAR AND LIVE

I have a deep heart's desire for everyone to hear the voice of the Lord. The Lord filled me with this desire when He commanded me to write this book. I have a dream about this happening in churches around the world. I have studied a passage from Deuteronomy over and over and each time it inspires me to seek to be in a place where this offer is made again.

> *"So it was, when you heard the voice from the midst of the darkness, while the mountain was burning with fire, that you came near to me, all the heads of your tribes and your elders. And you said: 'Surely the Lord our God has shown us His glory and His greatness, and we have heard His voice from the midst of the fire. We have seen this day that God speaks with man; yet he still lives. Now therefore, why should we die? For this great fire will consume us; if we hear the voice of the Lord our God anymore, then we shall die. For who is there of all flesh who has heard the voice of the living God speaking from the midst of the fire, as we have, and lived? You go near and hear*

*all that the Lord our God may say, and tell us all
that the Lord our God says to you, and we will
hear and do it.'"* (Deuteronomy 5:23-27)

Can you picture this in your mind? The Lord invited the
entire community to come close and hear His voice. Wow! Is
that invitation still available? I believe it is. And I pray with
all the love that is within me that you will not respond like the
people did in Moses' day. Can you imagine refusing to listen
to the audible voice of the Lord? Every time I hear His audible
voice, my spirit and soul jump with joy. What an awesome gift!
What an awesome opportunity! I want to turn the volume up
for everyone!

INCREASE THE VOLUME OF YOUR WITNESS

This is the other side of the volume issue. How loudly are
you witnessing for the Lord? Are you willing to shout from
the housetops? Are you willing to go into the highways and
byways to proclaim the gospel of the kingdom? Are you ready
to hear the voice of the Lord and share His words with others?
I will not try to deceive you. It is true that there is a price to be
paid. You may find as I did that some of your friends will no
longer want to be associated with you. In faith, you must trust
that the Lord will send more friends who are more compatible
with your experience in the Lord. That certainly happened for
me. Remember:

> *"For the testimony of Jesus is the spirit of proph-
> ecy."* (Revelation 19:10b)

Many people are not listening for the voice of the Lord
because no one has shared with them that it is supposed to be
the norm rather than the exception. No one has let the testimony of their lives be a prophetic word about how the Lord

wants to speak to them. They may never have met anyone who has heard the voice of the Lord and lived to tell about it. That fear of judgment still holds people back from the fullness of the blessing. I stand on my decrees to cast out every spirit of fear from the family of God. I want people free to hear and respond to our awesome Father God. After all, is there a good father on Earth who refuses to speak to his children? No way! So why do we fear that our Father in Heaven does not want to speak to His children any longer? What kind of image of a loving God is this? Of course our loving Father gives good things to us! Remember:

> *"Do not be deceived, my beloved brethren. Every good gift and every perfect gift is from above, and comes down from the Father of lights, with whom there is no variation or shadow of turning. Of His own will He brought us forth by the word of truth, that we might be a kind of firstfruits of His creatures. So then, my beloved brethren, let every man be swift to hear, slow to speak, slow to wrath."* (James 1:16-19)

We are to be the first-fruits of His new creation. He didn't do this so that we can remain like everyone else in the world, but that we might be new; with new gifts and a new anointing. Amen!

> *"There He made a statute and an ordinance for them, and there He tested them, and said, 'If you diligently heed the voice of the Lord your God and do what is right in His sight, give ear to His commandments and keep all His statutes, I will put none of the diseases on you which I have brought on the Egyptians. For I am the Lord who heals you.'"* (Exodus 15:25b-26)

How can you "diligently heed the voice of the Lord" if you can't hear it? God doesn't set up traps for us. He doesn't give us tasks which cannot be performed. He is always there to enable, gift, and bless us. He gives good and perfect gifts. Trust Him! Listen to Him! Obey His voice so that you will continue to hear!

ADDITIONAL SCRIPTURES FOR FURTHER STUDY

"Then it came to pass on the third day, in the morning, that there were thunderings and lightnings, and a thick cloud on the mountain; and the sound of the trumpet was very loud, so that all the people who were in the camp trembled. And Moses brought the people out of the camp to meet with God, and they stood at the foot of the mountain. Now Mount Sinai was completely in smoke, because the Lord descended upon it in fire. Its smoke ascended like the smoke of a furnace, and the whole mountain quaked greatly. And when the blast of the trumpet sounded long and became louder and louder, Moses spoke, and God answered him by voice. Then the Lord came down upon Mount Sinai, on the top of the mountain. And the Lord called Moses to the top of the mountain, and Moses went up." (Exodus 19:16-20)

"Now all the people witnessed the thunderings, the lightning flashes, the sound of the trumpet, and the mountain smoking; and when the people saw it, they trembled and stood afar off. Then they said to Moses, 'You speak with us, and we will hear; but let not God speak with us, lest we

die.' And Moses said to the people, 'Do not fear; for God has come to test you, and that His fear may be before you, so that you may not sin.' So the people stood afar off, but Moses drew near the thick darkness where God was. Then the Lord said to Moses, 'Thus you shall say to the children of Israel: "You have seen that I have talked with you from heaven."'" (Exodus 20:18-22)

"Even those from afar shall come and build the temple of the Lord. Then you shall know that the Lord of hosts has sent Me to you. And this shall come to pass if you diligently obey the voice of the Lord your God." (Zechariah 6:15)

"Also I heard the voice of the Lord, saying: 'Whom shall I send, And who will go for Us?' Then I said, 'Here am I! Send me.' And He said, 'Go, and tell this people: "Keep on hearing, but do not understand; Keep on seeing, but do not perceive."'" (Isaiah 6:8-9)

"The voice of the Lord is over the waters; The God of glory thunders; The Lord is over many waters. The voice of the Lord is powerful; The voice of the Lord is full of majesty." (Psalm 29:3-4)

PRAYER

"Finally, my brethren, be strong in the Lord and in the power of His might. Put on the whole armor of God, that you may be able to stand against the wiles of the devil. For we do not wrestle against flesh and blood, but against principalities, against powers, against the rulers of the darkness of this age, against spiritual *hosts* of wickedness in the heavenly *places*. Therefore take up the whole armor of God, that you may be able to withstand in the evil day, and having done all, to stand. Stand therefore, having girded your waist with truth, having put on the breastplate of righteousness, and having shod your feet with the preparation of the gospel of peace; above all, taking the shield of faith with which you will be able to quench all the fiery darts of the wicked one. And take the helmet of salvation, and the sword of the Spirit, which is the word of God; praying always with all prayer and supplication in the Spirit, being watchful to this end with all perseverance and supplication for all the saints—and for me, that utterance may be given to me, that I may open my mouth boldly to make known the mystery of the gospel." (Ephesians 6:10-19)

CHAPTER 10

BECOME VIRULENT VEGETATION

―⁓⁓◆⁓⁓―

Once again, I found myself standing before the ancient door into the Secret Place of the Most High. I had learned on previous visits that there was nothing for me to do in front of this door except to wait on the Lord. No human effort can open the door to the Secret Place of the Most High God. Only the Holy Spirit is able to open that door for us. So, I waited! Thankfully, I didn't have to wait very long. The thorny vines in front of the door parted as the Holy Spirit once again opened up the passage into the Secret Place for me. I moved in with reverence and awe, knelt on the floor in worship, and waited for instructions from the Holy Spirit.

On this visit, the cloud of God's presence was noticeably absent. However, before I could spend time thinking about it or trying to understand why it was absent, the Holy Spirit guided me up the steps to the next level. I always like going to the next level. How about you?

This level was truly awesome and majestic. I stood gazing into the night sky which was totally free from clouds, haze, or ambient light. In the natural, all of these tend to blur our heavenly view. I looked in awe at the stars majestically positioned and was amazed by my ability to see through the darkness as if it were daylight. Then I heard the voice of the Lord again saying, "Come up here!"

At this command, I was immediately transported into the

Lord's presence in Heaven. I fell prostrate before the Lord in worship, awe, and holy fear. The Lord reached out His hand and lifted me up and stood me on my feet once again. Somehow, it seemed awkward to be standing before the holiness and majesty of the Lord. However, I was determined to be obedient even as every fiber of my being urged me to fall before His mighty presence. In this moment, I began to feel even more filled with awe at the mighty God who loved me enough to let me stand in His presence.

The Lord did not waste any time getting down to business. This experience was not some guided tour of Heaven to let me feel this sense of awe. It was not even given to inspire me in some esoteric experience. There was obviously business to be conducted on this visit. I soon learned that this was going to be another extended training session. On previous visits, the Lord had been giving me instructions for this book and what actions I was to take after receiving His instructions. The titles for all 12 chapters were given to me by the Lord and I also received an outline for each of the chapters over a period of 2-3 weeks.

When the Lord gave the title for this chapter, I was somewhat stunned and struggled to understand His words. He said, "Become Virulent Vegetation!" I knew what *vegetation* meant and I understood the word *virulent*. However, I had never heard the two words connected together. So I asked the Lord to help me understand. Then he said something even more confusing for me. He said, "Become kingdom kudzu!" I knew that I was going to need lots of help with this chapter and these instructions. So I waited on the Lord to release wisdom and revelation. What follows is a summary of the teaching the Lord gave me on that visit to the Secret Place.

However, before launching into this teaching, I want to point out that this chapter is related to the revelation the Lord provided to Bill Bright, Loren Cunningham, and Dr. Francis Shaffer in the fall of 1975. The word the Lord gave to these three individuals (at approximately the same time) in visions and revelation concerned the seven dimensions of all cultures. We are currently engaged in spiritual warfare in all of these dimensions. Each is, in effect, a battleground for the souls of all mankind. These seven dimensions of culture—which became known as the seven mountains of culture—were fore-shadowed in the seven enemies Israel faced when they went into the Promised Land. Then, as now, the task of the Lord's people is to establish a kingdom on Earth for our God.

Since the giving of this revelation, many leaders have further developed and taught the concepts and principles of this mandate from the Lord. I have studied many of the teachings from these leaders and attended several conferences in which these revelations have been taught. One thread that runs through all of these teachings is that, as a result of the fall in the Garden of Eden and the subsequent failures of all mankind, these mountains of culture have become occupied by the enemy. On the top of each mountain, a prince demon rules over those who are aligned with and serving in one of these seven areas of our culture. Most, if not all, human occupations (jobs) relate to one or more of these mountains. These seven aspects of all cultures have been identified as: family, church, education, media, arts and entertainment, economy (business), and government. The order in which these are listed varies from writer to writer.

Another common theme among these theorists is that God calls us to take these mountains back for the Lord. As we reclaim the mountains of culture, we will begin to return the Nations to the Lord one by one. In my spirit, I began to understand that the Lord wants each of us to rise up like Caleb and in the spirit of Caleb declare:

> *"And now, behold, the LORD has kept me alive, as He said, these forty-five years, ever since the LORD spoke this word to Moses while Israel wandered in the wilderness; and now, here I am this*

*day, eighty-five years old. As yet I am as strong this day as on the day that Moses sent me; just as my strength was then, so now is my strength for war, both for going out and for coming in. Now therefore, **give me this mountain** of which the LORD spoke in that day; for you heard in that day how the Anakim were there, and that the cities were great and fortified. It may be that the LORD will be with me, and I shall be able to drive them out as the LORD said." (Joshua 14:10-12)*

Caleb was not discouraged by his age, even though he was now 85 years old. He had no fear because he had never wavered in his trust for the Lord. He saw what others had failed to see. These battles are the Lord's battles and He will always be with His people. Caleb was further blessed in that his strength had remained with him this entire time. Caleb was not afraid of the giants on his first visit to this land, and he was not afraid of them in his later years. He had a mandate from God to take Hebron and he would not be deterred by danger or difficulties. This is the attitude all warriors in the kingdom of God should maintain. When David faced Goliath he, like Caleb centuries before, understood whose battle it was and testified:

"Then David said to the Philistine, 'You come to me with a sword, with a spear, and with a javelin. But I come to you in the name of the LORD of hosts, the God of the armies of Israel, whom you have defied. This day the LORD will deliver you into my hand, and I will strike you and take your head from you. And this day I will give the carcasses of the camp of the Philistines to the birds of the air and the wild beasts of the earth, that all the earth may know that there is a God in Israel. Then all this assembly shall know that the

LORD *does not save with sword and spear; for the*
battle is the LORD's, *and He will give you into our*
hands.'" (1 Samuel 17:45-47)

Today, the Lord is looking for a few good men and women
who will rise up and take a stand for the kingdom of God. He is
calling for men and women to take back the mountains of our
culture by defeating the giants, the demonic principalities and
demonic spirits which reside there. The task is not easy and the
danger is real. But we must never forget that it is God's battle.
We must take heart in the knowledge that He is with us and will
never leave us or forsake us. We must believe what the Lord
proclaimed at least 238 times in scripture – Do not be afraid!
The Lord still calls on His people to cast off fear, be strong and
courageous, and fight the good fight of faith. Are you ready to
take your place in the Lord's army?

I like these teachings about the seven mountains and love to
hear them over and over. However, I began to notice that when
I got motivated and was ready to rise to the challenge, something was missing. I soon learned what was out of focus for
me. I wanted to know, "What is my specific mission? Which
mountain am I called to take back or help take back for the
Lord?" The theories are all general and lack these specifics.

The Lord made me aware that this will always be the case,
because only He can reveal to you which mountain you are to
take and how you are to accomplish the tasks He is assigning
to you. This is why the Lord wants each of us to come up to
the Third Heaven. He wants us to come up so that He can teach
each of us our specific mission and direct us to the mountain of
our calling. Be prepared, because these assignments can shift.
David was first called to the economy or business mountain
where he worked at a very low level position as a shepherd
over his father's sheep. As he was proven strong and courageous, the Lord suddenly shifted him to the top of the government mountain where he replaced Saul as king.

God spoke very specifically to me about wanting people to visit the Third Heaven, where they could be trained and commissioned by Him for specific duty on the mountain of their calling. He wants to make this very clear to each of us. You simply cannot get these instructions from any other source or any other person. They must come from the Lord. Not everyone is willing to courageously step out and face the giants on their assigned mountain. Please be aware: this is one of the reasons some have not visited the Third Heaven as of yet.

It is God's grace to wait until He knows that people are ready to be obedient to His calling. He does not want us to visit Heaven prematurely and, as a result of disobedience, come under judgment. If you haven't made a visit to Heaven yet, consider this and examine yourself to see if your unwillingness to obey the Lord may be holding you back. Instead of being upset that it hasn't worked for you, perhaps it is time to thank God that He didn't put you into a position of jeopardy. We must each face the big question: Are you truly willing to obey the Lord no matter how challenging the assignment may be or which giant may occupy your mountain?

As you have probably noticed in many other teachings, the message of this chapter is not to provide you with the specifics of your assignment. I want to reemphasize that you must visit the Lord and receive them directly from Him. The purpose of this chapter is to help you gain an understanding of some general principles for taking a mountain for the Lord.

In the beginning of this chapter, I shared that the Lord told me that we must, "Be virulent vegetation! Become kingdom kudzu!" If you are not from the southern part of the United States, you may be wondering, "What is kudzu?"

Kudzu is an extremely virulent plant which was introduced into the United States in 1876 as both an ornamental plant and an excellent ground cover. In the mid 1930s, after an extended time of drought, it was used to keep the soil from splitting open and causing great damage to crop producing areas of the southeastern United States. The plant was imported from Japan and named kudzu after the word "kuzu," which is the Japanese name for the plant.

This plant—which was native to Japan, Korea, and southeastern China—quickly spread, especially in the southeastern part of the United States where the conditions are truly ideal for its rapid growth. In this area, it spread so quickly that by 1953 it was officially labeled as a pest weed by the US Department of Agriculture. It is virtually impossible to eradicate this plant, whose rapid growth gave it a variety of nicknames such as the "foot-a-night vine" and the "mile-a-minute vine." This plant has no natural predators and costs the United States several million dollars per year in control measures.

Kudzu has many positive benefits. Kudzu is a legume and benefits the soil by raising the nitrogen level, resulting in increased fertility. Its very deep taproots bring minerals from deep underground to the surface where they actually improve the topsoil. Kudzu can be used to feed livestock. The vines, leaves and roots of the plant have many nutritional benefits and are currently being used in the development of many health foods and medicines. The many known health benefits from the various parts of this plant range from the treatment of migraine headaches to diarrhea. It has also been used in the development of medications for the treatment of many different types of allergies.

Despite these benefits, kudzu is a pest weed because it can so rapidly spread and destroy forests, crops, and manmade structures. As you drive through the southeastern part of the United States, you see kudzu growing quickly to cover fences, trees, and electrical poles. After a short time, the original plants or structures are so heavily covered that their original identity is lost under the huge growth of this weed.

As I repeatedly drove along the interstate highway through the state of Mississippi over a period of a few weeks, I noticed one particular electrical pole that was being overgrown by kudzu. At first, I could still make out the outline of the pole. Then the kudzu became so thick that all I could see was the plant. As it grew over and around the pole and its crossbars, it began to take on the shape of the pole and it eventually looked like a giant green cross.

As I looked at this cross made up of a virulent form of vegetation, I received a revelation which helped me to understood what the Lord was saying when He decreed that we should become "Kingdom Kudzu." We are to spread so rapidly up the mountains that the enemy does not have the time or resources to stop the constant increase of our covering. As we continue to move toward the top of the mountain, its appearance will begin to change. There will be a huge shift on the mountain's surface as the look of the cross of Jesus Christ covers over all the sin which has dominated the mountain. The victory will be won by a fast moving and persistent taking of territory for the Lord. As it happens, the mountain will look more and more like the people of God and less and less like the kingdom of Satan.

Kingdom carriers are being called forth to rapidly spread the kingdom of God covering the ground; covering the structures; and covering the signs and symbols of the enemy's authority. Before the enemy's forces know what is happening, the whole mountain will reflect the redeeming power of the cross of Christ. We are to literally cover the worldly kingdoms and replace them with the structures of God's kingdom. At first, the old structures and cultural icons will still be recognizable, but soon you will only see the kingdom of God. Fully equipped kingdom carriers will spread like kudzu. They will become virulent kingdom vegetation!

We might wonder why the enemy will allow this to happen. Why will he stand by as the virulent vegetation begins to rapidly spread? Like kudzu, it will be apparent that there are very important side benefits from the presence of these kingdom carriers. As people are healed, restored, built up, and made fit for service, the benefits will far outweigh the potential long-term effects. Those placed there by the Lord will be viewed as the answers to big problems, and by the time the danger to the enemy is apparent, it will be too late.

Another unfortunate characteristic of kudzu is that the seeds can lie dormant for years before they begin to grow. An area which seems to be successfully cleared of kudzu will suddenly breakout again with a new and virulent growth of the plant. To those trying to control it, it becomes quickly apparent that it cannot be stopped. Those who are called to carry the kingdom will have the same characteristics. Any notion that they have been stopped will soon be shown to have been a false hope. What appeared to be dead will rise again and move higher and higher up the mountain.

Kingdom carriers will be unstoppable. The enemy may attack violently and seem to have a victory. But the kingdom carriers will rise again and continue their work to cover the Earth and restore all things to our creator God and king.

February 11, 2011

On a cold February morning, I was surprised when my prayers suddenly changed in tone. As I prayed intercessory prayers for Israel, I was concerned about the movement of the Muslim Brotherhood to take over all the nations surrounding Israel. I was concerned that our government was apparently helping them with this takeover in the Middle East. This organization has made its intentions clear for a long time. They are adamantly committed to the destruction of Israel, the establishment of a world-wide caliphate, and to rule the world. Long ago, they published their charter on the web and made their intentions clear. This takeover in several neighboring nations is a serious threat to Israel's peace and security. As a result, my usual prayers for Israel were not coming out. I found myself praying military prayers. I prayed to our Commander in Chief to give orders to His soldiers on the frontlines of this present spiritual warfare. I prayed for the Lord to take command of His army, which was drawn up in battle lines against that ancient enemy and the host of evil backing up his threats. I asked to hear what Heaven is saying TODAY to the warriors of the Lord's army.

After I was lifted up into His presence, I looked down from Heaven on a great battlefield which had been formed on Earth. The clash of battle from both sides was awesome and casualties were mounting up rapidly. As I watched, both sides drew up their battle lines and dug in. The scene began to look like World War I trench warfare and both sides were getting hammered by small arms fire, grenades, and artillery. In spite of the casualties, both sides were hunkered down behind their trenches and hoping to be missed by the bombs bursting in the air. Even though they were getting hammered over and over, no one made a move. Both sides were immobilized in their trenches while enduring the onslaught that was taking its toll on every side.

I remembered the words of Psalm 91:

> *"A thousand may fall at your side, and ten thousand at your right hand; but it shall not come near you. Only with your eyes shall you look, and see the reward of the wicked. Because you have made the Lord, who is my refuge, even the Most High, your dwelling place, No evil shall befall you, nor shall any plague come near your dwelling; For He shall give His angels charge over you, to keep you in all your ways."* (Psalm 91:7-11)

Then I saw the mighty warring angels being released from Heaven and with great speed they reached the Lord's army lined up in the trenches. As they arrived, I heard the Lord say, "The time for building fortifications and holding your ground is past! You will continue to take casualties as long as you hide behind your weak defenses. It is time to move out! It is time to take the battle to the enemy! It is time to take back all the territory which belongs to the Lord and His saints." I remembered the words of the Lord to Joshua.

> *"Every place that the sole of your foot will tread upon I have given you, as I said to Moses. From the wilderness and this Lebanon as far as the great river, the River Euphrates, all the land of the Hittites, and to the Great Sea toward the going down of the sun, shall be your territory. No man shall be able to stand before you all the days of your life; as I was with Moses, so I will be with you. I will not leave you nor forsake you. Be strong and of good courage, for to this people you shall divide as an inheritance the land which I swore to their fathers to give them."* (Joshua 1:3-6)

Sometimes we act as if these words were easy for Joshua and Israel to hear, but not reassuring enough for you and me. We act as if we are holding the lines and God is waiting for some future day to move His army into battle. I heard the Lord say, "Stop hiding behind your fortifications. Be strong and courageous for I am with you! Rise up, now!" It is hard to stand up and move out when bullets are flying! But it is more dangerous to hide in a trench and be hammered by enemy fire. Then I heard the Lord command, "Charge!" At this command, the mighty men and women arose from the trenches and ran to the battle. Others who were more fearful were encouraged by those who stood up first and soon followed. Then I took heart in the promises of Psalm 91:1-6,

> *"He who dwells in the secret place of the Most High shall abide under the shadow of the Almighty. I will say of the Lord, 'He is my refuge*

and my fortress; my God, in Him I will trust.'
Surely He shall deliver you from the snare of the
fowler and from the perilous pestilence. He shall
cover you with His feathers, and under His wings
you shall take refuge; His truth shall be your
shield and buckler. You shall not be afraid of the
terror by night, nor of the arrow that flies by day,
nor of the pestilence that walks in darkness, nor
of the destruction that lays waste at noonday."

What about you? Do you take heart in these words? If so, it is time to get out of the fortress and face a defeated enemy with an army of angels at your side! Are you ready? Are you willing to fight the good fight of faith? Are you ready to take your stand for the kingdom of God and when you have done all to stand, keep on standing? I am ready! Can you hear the command, "CHARGE!"? May we rise above our fears and our clinging to the threads of this life and embrace life eternal! Amen!

"For He shall give His angels charge over you,
to keep you in all your ways. In their hands they
shall bear you up, lest you dash your foot against
a stone. You shall tread upon the lion and the
cobra, the young lion and the serpent you shall
trample underfoot." (Psalm 91:11-13)

Remember the words of Paul in 2 Corinthians 10:3-6,

"For though we walk in the flesh, we do not
war according to the flesh. For the weapons of
our warfare are not carnal but mighty in God
for pulling down strongholds, casting down ar-
guments and every high thing that exalts itself
against the knowledge of God, bringing every

thought into captivity to the obedience of Christ,
and being ready to punish all disobedience when
your obedience is fulfilled."

We do not war against flesh and blood. So our weapons are not the weapons of worldly warfare. Our greatest weapon is love! Love armed with the Word of God (the sword) seeks to deliver those who are captives of the enemy. "Bless and do not curse!" "Love your enemies!" "Do good to those who persecute you and despitefully use you!" When we can do this, the enemy (that ancient enemy – the devil) will be destroyed before our eyes. Amen!

PRAYER

"When Your people go out to battle against their enemies, wherever You send them, and when they pray to You toward this city which You have chosen and the temple which I have built for Your name, then hear from Heaven their prayer and their supplication, and maintain their cause. (2 Chronicles 6:34-35)

CHAPTER 11

RECEIVING A KINGDOM VOCABULARY

"Then He said to them, 'Therefore every scribe instructed concerning the kingdom of heaven is like a householder who brings out of his treasure things new and old.'" (Matthew 13:52)

My face time with the Lord began with an open vision. In the vision, I stood in a doorway and watched several front doors in the neighborhood open as people emerged early in the morning. It was very bright, sunny, and warm outside the houses in this vision and people were stepping out into a new day filled with great promise.

My mind reflected on the promise in Psalm 30:

"Sing praise to the Lord, you saints of His, And give thanks at the remembrance of His holy name. For His anger is but for a moment, His favor is for life; Weeping may endure for a night, But joy comes in the morning." (Psalm 30:4-5)

The clear message I was receiving today was that it is time to stop weeping over what seems lost in the past and to begin to move out into the new thing the Lord has prepared for us. I was given another scripture.

> *"Then He who sat on the throne said, 'Behold,*
> *I make all things new.' And He said to me,*
> *'Write, for these words are true and faithful.'"*
> (Revelation 21:5)

The Lord is faithful and His words and promises are true. Now is the time to embrace the new thing which He is birthing in you, your family, and your ministry. Amen!

As I was reflecting on these things, I was carried in the Spirit to another place. I found myself standing in front of an elevator. I had a bookshelf with me which was mounted on wheels like those in a library. When the elevator doors opened, I stepped in, pulling my library with me. As I leaned forward to push the button for my floor, I noticed that there was only one destination available: Heaven! I liked that and began to be filled with expectancy as I rose higher and higher toward my goal – His presence.

Then something strange began to happen. One by one, the books began to float up out of the shelves and disappear. By the time the door opened in Heaven, the shelves were empty. I didn't bother to pull the shelves with me. The books were all gone and the shelves now had no value.

I asked for understanding and the Holy Spirit revealed to me that we have to leave everything behind. I knew that these were the last things I wanted to leave behind. (Notice: I'm talking about things and not people. The people I care about will also be in Heaven.) It seemed like all I had studied and learned was now too insignificant to be carried into Heaven. Then the realization came that it is not about what I know, what I think, or what I have done. It is about Him and about being in His presence.

After exiting the elevator, I was now standing in a long hallway and saw several people moving about in both directions. I felt led to turn to my right, believing that this was the way to go in order for me to move into the Lord's presence. I walked for a very long distance in the hallway without finding my destination.

Then something really strange came into my mind. I suddenly wanted to find a "Starbucks" coffee shop. In a very short period of time the hallway opened into a large area which looked like a coffee shop. The outside wall was made of glass and Sonlight filled the room. Many people were gathered at small tables sharing stories. I noticed that there was so much joy in all of their faces. There were also several people at the coffee counter waiting for their orders to be filled so they could join the other people at their tables.

When my order came, I joined a group of people I had never seen before. Even though we had never met, we immediately felt connected. We were all family! That was a really good feeling. As I joined the conversation, I realized that everyone was sharing testimonies about what Jesus had done in their lives. With each story, everyone's joy grew stronger. I felt such awesome peace – the Shalom of God was so strong here. I thought of Revelation 19:10, "For the testimony of Jesus is the spirit of prophecy." We were literally prophesying ourselves up into a higher realm of joy as we basked in the warmth of His light all around us.

I realized that, as I had left behind all the bad experiences of life, my level of peace and joy had increased. As I left behind the good things I had held on to, my level had increased again, perhaps even more dramatically. I left behind the good things to get into the realm of the best things! I believe that the Lord wants to release an impartation for us to leave behind all the things (good and bad) which hinder our walk with Him and move into a higher realm of His glory. He wants us to do that so we can experience His love at a new and much greater depth! Are you ready to leave behind everything which hinders and move into the realm of His glory? If your answer is "Yes!" this impartation is for you!

RESISTANCE TO CHANGE

"Then He who sat on the throne said, 'Behold, I make all things new.' And He said to me, 'Write, for these words are true and faithful.'" (Revelation 21:5)

I have always been amazed at the resistance of the church to new things. Innovators of new ideas—even those received directly from the Lord—have often been martyred for their faithful service. Wars have been fought over small changes in doctrine or practice. How can a group whose primary mandate is "love" resort to killing people for the purity of their ideas? Yet it happens all the time, and it has been happening throughout human history. Remember what they did to Jesus for bringing a fresh word from the Father.

"And He entered the synagogue again, and a man was there who had a withered hand. So they watched Him closely, whether He would heal him on the Sabbath, so that they might accuse Him. And He said to the man who had the withered hand, 'Step forward.' Then He said to them, 'Is it lawful on the Sabbath to do good or to do evil, to save life or to kill?' But they kept silent. And when He had looked around at them with anger, being grieved by the hardness of their hearts, He said to the man, 'Stretch out your hand.' And he stretched it out, and his hand was restored as whole as the other. Then the Pharisees went out and immediately plotted with the Herodians against Him, how they might destroy Him." (Mark 3:1-6)

I used to hear something over and over during my time in

the Army. They would say, "No good deed goes unpunished!" I don't know the origin of this old saying, but it seems to be true in many cases. Every bureaucracy seems to have the same prime directive to protect all of its ideas and processes from every attempt at change. After thinking about it for a while, I decided that perhaps we can actually trace this idiom back to something Jesus said. Perhaps this idiom began when Jesus said:

"Then the Jews took up stones again to stone Him. Jesus answered them, 'Many good works I have shown you from My Father. For which of those works do you stone Me?'" (John 10:31-32)

Churches are often more willing to repeat a program which has failed to produce positive results for the last several years rather than stepping out in faith to try something new. Much of this is from a fear of the unknown. Some of it comes from concern that something new will take more work and require more time. But my experience has been that most of these programs are identified with some specific person whom people fear to face when their pet project is no longer being used or has been altered.

In one church I pastored, I was taken by a group of deacons to the house of an aging innovator and severely criticized for trying new things. There was something like a spirit of dread which came over the entire group when changes were proposed. They were so afraid of offending this one person that the church had become immobilized. The interesting twist was that this man was in favor of change. That was how the previous program had begun. This unwillingness to change is a tragic state for the church. A church can never move ahead and stay in step with the Kingdom of God as long as it is paralyzed in fear. I have discovered that the fear of man is the source of so much of the resistance and many of the failures in the church.

To avoid things we fear, we keep doing the same things over

and over, whether they work or not. Yet, the scriptures point clearly to the fact that God is doing new things all the time. Consider the following representative scripture references.

> *"Do not remember the former things, nor con-*
> *sider the things of old. Behold, I will do a new*
> *thing, now it shall spring forth; shall you not*
> *know it?"* (Isaiah 43:18-19a)

> *"How long will you gad about, O you backslid-*
> *ing daughter? For the* LORD *has created a new*
> *thing in the earth—A woman shall encompass a*
> *man."* (Jeremiah 31:22)

> *"Then He who sat on the throne said, 'Behold, I*
> *make all things new.' And He said to me, 'Write,*
> *for these words are true and faithful.'"* (Revela-
> tion 21:5)

If we think about it for a moment, anything other than changing when the Lord shifts would seem foolish. If we are to become more like Him, we should consider who He is. How could a creator God stop being creative? How could a creative God do anything except produce new things all the time? It is in God's very nature to do new things, and He created us in His own image. We were made to be creative and to attempt new things constantly. At the heart of our nature, we have been formed to enjoy new things and to celebrate the adventure of exploring all the exciting things our Father God has made and continues to create. If we get stuck in one of the old things as God moves forward, we will find ourselves further and further from where He is and where He has called us to be.

Nine times the Bible instructs us to sing a new song to the Lord, but try to get that past a church committee. People hold on to old songs for nostalgic reasons. I think I have heard all of the so-called reasons. I am painfully reminded of a few. "It was my mother's favorite song and we have to keep singing it even if we don't know what the old language means!" "If these songs were good enough for Jesus and Paul, they are good enough for me!" "Who cares what the young people want? This is our church and we will do it our way! If they don't like it, they can leave!" No wonder we have experienced a mass exodus of the youth from traditional churches!

Even in Heaven, there will be new songs of praise. If you can't stand new songs here, you should pick a different eternal destiny, because Heaven is filled with new songs and new things! New songs are mentioned twice in the book of Revelation as something which will be done in Heaven. And we are commanded to sing new songs while we are still on the Earth.

> *"'I am the Lord, that is My name; And My glory I will not give to another, Nor My praise to carved images. Behold, the former things have come to pass, And new things I declare; Before they spring forth I tell you of them.' Sing to the Lord a new song, And His praise from the ends of the earth, You who go down to the sea, and all that is in it, You coastlands and you inhabitants of them!"* (Isaiah 42:8-10)

We obviously need a great deal of help to obey the Lord in this area of new things. But don't worry. The Lord has provided a solution. He has sent a helper! He has sent a guide to lead us into all these new things. If it causes you pain, don't worry. He is also the comforter. I pray that we will seek His help to change as God changes and move into His new things! Amen!

> *"I still have many things to say to you, but you cannot bear them now. However, when He, the*

Spirit of truth, has come, He will guide you into all truth; for He will not speak on His own authority, but whatever He hears He will speak; and He will tell you things to come. He will glorify Me, for He will take of what is Mine and declare it to you." (John 16:12-14)

All those new things which God is doing require us to constantly develop new words as we attempt to describe how the Lord is moving today. Most of our old language is simply inadequate to convey the new ideas and describe the new phenomena. So where do you go to get this new vocabulary? Let me caution you that it is not necessarily the vocabulary being taught by others. I went that way first with this lesson.

I was impressed by the new language I was hearing from some young evangelists and pastors. I thought that perhaps this was what the Lord had meant in the title of this chapter. But as I continued to listen to these young warriors, I noticed that they were shifting constantly. The catch words for this season have little or no meaning in the next season.

It was clear to me that I was about to make the mistake of trying to institutionalize the new language and hold on to it until it became old. The real lesson here is about how the young men and women in these last days seem to have a nature to embrace change. I want to embrace that same willingness to change and always be ready to move when the Lord moves. How about you?

I went back to what Jesus taught:

"Then He said to them, 'Therefore every scribe instructed concerning the kingdom of heaven is like a householder who brings out of his treasure things new and old.'" (Matthew 13:52)

If the Lord is releasing new words, we need to get this

vocabulary directly from the Holy Spirit. I had an old mentor in the army who constantly said, "Use words they don't understand, and then you get a chance to explain it before they can take it [funding or personnel] away." New words catch people's attention, and we can use the new vocabulary to get them to listen to the "old, old story" about Jesus. This story never actually becomes old. It is made new in every season and in every generation as people are being born again in the Spirit.

WHEN THE OLD BECOMES NEW

Don't be surprised if your "new" vocabulary is someone else's familiar vocabulary. The Lord taught me a wonderful lesson about this in a series of Third Heaven Training visits. For a more complete explanation of one of these old things becoming new, read the message about impartation at the end of the book. What the Lord began to reveal to me more and more was the hidden power of the Hebrew language. I received a word from the Holy Spirit that Hebrew is the perfect language to release knowledge and understanding about the things of the Kingdom of God. It is the language the Lord created and gave to His anointed people so that He could disclose Himself more fully to them. This word came to me a few years ago and I have been interested to discover that many other people are teaching this same idea. We have the same Holy Spirit and the same Lord. It should be no surprise when He gives the same message to others. The good news is that we all belong to the same Father God who wants to give us new things and perfect things every day.

When the Lord revealed this to me, I began a long series of research projects to learn the meaning of Hebrew numbers, letters, words, and phrases. I subscribed to several teaching newsletters being sent out by Rabbis, Messianic Pastors, and Hebrew scholars. Several times a week, I get a major revelation from one or more of these sources. Now, when I hear something which seems new from the Lord, I have a better point of reference for understanding the fullness of the revelation. I plan to continue to research and explore, because there has been so much fruit from every venture into Hebrew.

To help me learn more quickly, I play Messianic praise and worship songs on my computer as I do my Bible study, research and writing. Constantly hearing Hebrew in the songs and in spoken words helps me to anchor these words in my mind. It also assists me with improving my pronunciation of the Lord's key words for the season. I find that hearing the Hebrew language has helped to set a frame for the new things I am receiving from the Holy Spirit.

As I reflected on the message from scriptures I used earlier concerning new songs, I realized that I'm doing that all the time as I learn new Messianic worship songs. I have a secret hope that this will help me to learn some of the new songs in Heaven so I can praise Him along with the angels and other saints. How about you? Are you ready for new songs, new language, and new ideas?

PICTURES AS KINGDOM VOCABULARY

There is another old saying I want to use here: "A picture is worth a thousand words." The origin of this idiom is uncertain, but it was published in a couple of slightly different forms in the 1920s. It has been attributed to an old Chinese proverb: "One picture is worth ten thousand words." Whatever the origin may be, there is some profound truth in it. If you look carefully at a painting or photograph, many things begin to go through your mind. These thoughts may range from reflecting on a small detail which catches your attention to going beyond the words and music in trying to understand the heart of the one who created it.

Our Father God created us with the ability to see and to understand images and pictures. He created this as a very powerful means of anchoring memories. Perhaps this is why He was so adamant about the command to make no graven images which might lead us into idolatry.

> *"You shall not make for yourself a carved image—any likeness of anything that is in heaven above, or that is in the earth beneath, or that is in the water under the earth; you shall not bow down to them nor serve them. For I, the Lord your God, am a jealous God, visiting the iniquity of the fathers upon the children to the third and fourth generations of those who hate Me, but showing mercy to thousands, to those who love Me and keep My commandments."* (Exodus 20:4-6)

It didn't take long for people to come up with all kinds of reasons to disobey this command of the Lord. Judgment came quickly to those who offended. You see, the Lord knows how we learn and retain information. After all, He created us this way. He gave us this great power called memory and so many of our memories are stored as images or word pictures. The great symbols of the church were developed to help people anchor their thoughts on the Lord. During an age of widespread illiteracy, the church used pictures to teach Bible stories and Bible truths. They were called "icons."

As with all innovations, this led to war and many people are still consumed with anger about these pictures. Many think they are worshipped as idols. If they are used properly, this does not happen. Every real "icon" has part of the picture going outside the frame to clearly state that it is an attempt to understand things of God, but can never fully disclose His awesome person.

Because of this God-given power for mental imagery, we need to be very careful about what pictures and images we allow into our minds. The enemy loves to exploit this strength in God's people and turn it into a weakness. He cleverly sets a trap with sensual, violent, and twisted images to bring confusion and fear to our minds. This is one of the powerful reasons the church needs to take a stand against pornography and violent content in movies, books, and video games. The Lord warned us about this deadly trap set by the enemy.

> *"But take heed to yourselves, lest your hearts be weighed down with carousing, drunkenness, and cares of this life, and that Day come on you unexpectedly. For it will come as a snare on all those who dwell on the face of the whole earth. Watch therefore, and pray always that you may be counted worthy to escape all these things that will come to pass, and to stand before the Son of Man."* (Luke 21:34-36)

The Lord has a different plan for the use of our ability to use images. He wants to release visions, spiritual pictures, and revelations which will build us up, strengthen us, and comfort all our hurts. I believe this is one of the reasons we are seeing such a huge increase in the number of people who are seeing visions and receiving a seer anointing. The Lord is preparing us for the great end time harvest and He is releasing these powerful teachings through the work of His Holy Spirit. Remember the words of Joel which were quoted by Peter to explain what happened on the Day of Pentecost.

> *"And it shall come to pass afterward That I will pour out My Spirit on all flesh; Your sons and your daughters shall prophesy, Your old men shall dream dreams, Your young men shall see visions. And also on My menservants and on My maidservants I will pour out My Spirit in those days. "And I will show wonders in the heavens and in the earth: Blood and fire and pillars of*

smoke. The sun shall be turned into darkness, And the moon into blood, Before the coming of the great and awesome day of the Lord." (Joel 2:28-31)

Notice that this gift is made available for young and old, male and female, Jew and Gentile. Now is the time to pray for increase in this gifting. If you haven't been baptized in the Holy Spirit and enabled to operate in these gifts, ask the Lord to finish the work He began in you. Ask to receive what was promised in the Word:

"If you then, being evil, know how to give good gifts to your children, how much more will your heavenly Father give the Holy Spirit to those who ask Him!" (Luke 11:13)

FEELINGS AS KINGDOM VOCABULARY

As I studied human nature in order to be a more effective counselor, I learned that many memories have been stored as feelings. When we were very young (before we had learned to speak) memories were stored as feelings. These memories are very difficult for a counselor to deal with because there are no words attached to these experiences of hurt, abandonment, or loss. For many in the mental health field, this is an area filled with mysteries and problems which are too difficult to solve. Yet, much of our current behavior is based on these feeling images. Life decisions were made at an early age as a result of these events and feelings. We cannot afford to simply ignore such a powerful source of information about ourselves.

As I conducted thousands of marriage counseling sessions over the last 40 years, I discovered the poorest vocabulary in most adults is in the area of feelings. In order to use language to help people heal, it is important to be able to communicate in precise words about feelings. One exercise I used was to have them list all of the feeling words they could remember. To help with this process I gave them four areas for concentration. These areas were: happy, sad, angry, and afraid. I was always amazed by people who could only think of a few words to describe these four main areas of human emotions. No wonder we have so much difficulty communicating about our feelings. It might be instructive for you to do this exercise. Draw four columns on a sheet of paper and label them with the four words above. List all the words you know. If the lists are short or one particular list is shorter than others, perhaps you could profit from a study of feelings.

After many years of searching, I finally found the best source for this information. I am going to reveal that secret to you. I spent years finding this truth and now you can have in a minute. But please don't discount it because it is simple and seemingly easy. I learned this from Jesus. All I had to do was ask. It just took a lot of work and frustration to lead me to that point.

> *"I still have many things to say to you, but you cannot bear them now. However, when He, the Spirit of truth, has come, He will guide you into all truth; for He will not speak on His own authority, but whatever He hears He will speak; and He will tell you things to come."* (John 16:12-13)

The Holy Spirit was with you when you experienced all these feelings. He remembers all the things you may have repressed or forgotten. Don't be afraid to explore this area of your past. He will not put more on you than you can handle. Some of us are more ready to hear the truth than others. He will wait until you are ready. Jesus waited because the disciples were not ready to bear the whole truth. I pray this daily. I ask the Holy Spirit, "Please give me all the truth I can handle today! Tomorrow, when I am able to handle more, then please release it to me!" I want to resolve all the issues which may be a barrier to my relationship with the Lord. I want to be free from everything which may hinder my ability to listen to Him. I want to be free from everything which may hinder my Third Heaven visits.

Now, here is some good news! There are some good and awesome memories stored as feelings. It is wonderful to get at them and celebrate what the Lord was doing for you all the way back to the moment of your conception. As I prayed for revelation from these experiences, I learned some exciting things. It suddenly came back that my first Third Heaven visit happened when I was three years old. I have had an image in my mind for as long as I can remember which gave me so much peace. Recently, I saw a painting of someone's recent experience in Heaven. It was exactly the same as what I saw when I was three years old.

More recently, I got in touch with an early feeling of fear which I didn't understand. When I was somewhere around 3-4 years old I had an open vision which was like being translated to a former time. I watched as animals two by two went up a ramp and through a door. Each pair of animals was larger than the ones before. My family didn't attend church, and I didn't have a background in the Bible or Bible stories. I was frightened by the animals rather than realizing that I was watching the loading of Noah's Ark. I had cried out in fear and was severely punished by my Father's belt for waking my sister. The whole memory was caught up in the pain of this experience. Now, by the help of the Holy Spirit, I was enabled to separate out the fear and hurt to see what the Lord had given to me. Wow! I watched the animals getting onto Noah's Ark without having any Bible background. Isn't God awesome! Even then, He was preparing me for how He is using me now. I now take joy from that memory, and it encourages me to embrace the seer anointing even more firmly. It is my destiny and now I know it.

Perhaps you have visited the Third Heaven or had an open vision when you were too small to attach words to it. Now may be your time to ask the Holy Spirit to help you recall and be blessed by those things lost in the shadows of time. Children have a built-in anointing for Third Heaven visitation, visions, and spiritual experiences. Remember what Jesus said:

> *"But Jesus called them to Him and said, 'Let the little children come to Me, and do not forbid them; for of such is the kingdom of God. Assuredly, I say to you, whoever does not receive the kingdom of God as a little child will by no means enter it.'"* (Luke 18:16-17)

Who knows what hidden treasures you may have in your memories? Who knows what awesome insight and spiritual truths may be stored there? The Holy Spirit knows! Ask Him! Amen!

PRAYER

Father God, thank you for being with me all my life. Thank you that the Holy Spirit has always been present with me, even before I knew you. Thank you for giving me so many ways to learn about you and celebrate your goodness in my life. Father, help me to be open to every move you are making. Give me new songs, new ideas, and new vocabulary words to better describe who you are and what you are doing in my life. Thank you for memories of you from my childhood which I have not yet discovered. Thank you for knowing me and anointing me even while I was in my Mother's womb. I want to always follow you, please you, and bless you. Release the Holy Spirit to guide me, instruct me and reveal the truth to me! I give you praise, honor, glory and majesty for all the amazing things you do and the awesome characteristics of your person. I am constantly amazed by you and always in awe! May that awe and amazement never end! Amen and Amen!

CHAPTER 12

VISIONARIES SEE AND VALUE

As I neared the completion of this book on Third Heaven visitation, I felt very weighed down by all of the tasks needed to complete the final editing, cover designs, and paperwork for the contract with the publisher. As I went before the Lord, I struggled to put these things out of my mind so that I could enter into my time with Him. I was not very successful, and these things kept coming back into my thoughts. I felt like I was at a great distance from Heaven, but I was so hungry to be with the Lord. I repeatedly asked the Holy Spirit to help me. Then I realized that I was not alone. I was not really in my worship room. I was in an open vision from the Lord. I was in the company of many people longing to have Third Heaven visits but, like me this morning, they were so weighed down by the concerns of the world that it was difficult to break free and concentrate on the Lord. We were all praying for the same things. We were asking for the spiritual gifts needed to discern in the spirit and be drawn close to Him.

The Lord said to me, "I wanted you to experience what they are experiencing and to feel what they are feeling! Now let your spiritual eyes be open! I created you with spiritual eyes. They are real even if you are not using them. Now use them! Let your eyes see across the great spiritual distance and draw you into my presence!"

If you have been striving to have Third Heaven visits, this message is for you. I have a greater appreciation for how

234

difficult it is and how hard you are trying. But it isn't about trying harder or pressing in more. It is about relaxing in the presence of the Lord and just letting go of everything that hinders so that your eyes are open to the spiritual realm. It is about looking toward Heaven and letting yourself be drawn up into His presence. When I did this, it was amazing. It was like having telescopic eyes. It seemed like Heaven was drawn to me. Then I realized that I had been praying the promise in James 4:8, "Draw near to God and He will draw near to you!" Two things happened at the same time. I was drawn toward Him and Heaven was drawn near to me.

Suddenly, I was in the throne room in Heaven. Something was different on this visit from anything I had experienced before. I was in the middle of some sort of commissioning service. When I saw those being commissioned, I was stunned and stood in awe looking at them. They were not people or angels. They were some kind of creature or being from Heaven I had not seen before. The Lord said, "They are watchers being sent throughout the world!" My thoughts went to Daniel, Chapter 4:

> *"This decision is by the decree of the watchers,*
> *And the sentence by the word of the holy ones,*
> *In order that the living may know That the Most*
> *High rules in the kingdom of men, Gives it to*
> *whomever He will, And sets over it the lowest of*
> *men."* (Daniel 4:17)

The watchers looked strange and awesome to me. They were about 4 feet tall with leather-like skin on their heads. They had arms, legs, and a torso. However, that was the limit of their likeness to humans. What was really unusual was their eyes. It looked like they were wearing some type of dark glasses, but it looked as if these were part of their heads. The lenses of the glasses were very dark and I could not see eyes behind them. However, there were eyes all around the frames. An extension went up and above each of the frames, but was also part of the frames. Each of these extensions had three eyes. The watchers paraded by me as they departed Heaven. I looked closely at them, but I could not tell if they were looking at me or not. Each of them had something like a clipboard with paper for writing down what they observed. Each had a pen in the left hand.

I asked the Holy Spirit for wisdom to understand what I was seeing. The Spirit said, "These are watchers being sent out to watch over those who belong to the Lord. They are not being sent out to judge or condemn. They are watching those who need spiritual gifts and those who need to strengthen the gifts which they have already received."

I was powerfully reminded that we are living in a time of grace. The time of judgment and wrath has not yet come, but it is not far away. This is a time to receive spiritual gifts (especially discerning gifts), to strengthen gifts we already possess by using them, and to employ the gifts we have been given for the harvest. The Lord wants to release more to you and He is watching for the right moment when you are ready to receive these new things.

Part of this readiness is determined by what we are doing with the gifts we have already received. It is not a season to possess unused gifts. It is a time to increase gifting through using everything the Holy Spirit has already given. If you need help seeing in the spiritual realm, this is very good news.

Hear what the Lord said and then do it. "Now let your spiritual eyes be open! I created you with spiritual eyes. They are real even if you are not using them. Now, use them! Let your eyes see across the great spiritual distance and draw you into my presence!" Amen!

One additional revelation came from this experience in Heaven. We are only able to fully embrace and use the gifts which we truly value.

MEANING ONLY COMES FROM WHAT YOU VALUE

If you don't value a prophet, you cannot truly receive a prophetic word from him. If you don't value a teacher, you will not learn and retain what he is teaching. If you don't value an evangelist, it is unlikely that you will respond to the invitation to accept the Lord. If you don't believe someone has an apostolic anointing, you will not willingly follow his leadership. If you honestly reflect back on your own experiences, you will probably see and understand why you responded to some and did not to others.

The same is true of visions and Third Heaven visitation. If you don't respect and honor those who are teaching you, it is unlikely that you will experience an impartation from them. However, I want to take it further than this. If you do not respect and honor what the Lord gives you in a vision or spiritual encounter, you will not be led to receive understanding and revelation. I'll give you a very simple example.

I have been obeying the Lord for several years now to release impartation for Third Heaven visitation. Some people do not respect this anointing or me as a teacher. As a result, they limit their opportunities to experience what the Lord has for them. It is not about me. It is about valuing what the Lord wants to do for them and through them. Some people have immediately had very awesome Third Heaven visits. Their testimonies have inspired others who then approached with faith and experienced a visit of their own.

Here is an important truth: the Lord gives to each as He chooses based on their readiness and calling. Several people who have received this impartation report seeing only a purple or blue cloud. Some have been excited and filled with gratitude to the Lord for showing them His Shekinah glory. But some have responded with disappointment, anger, and resentment. They expected more and resented only receiving this small vision. Now think for a moment. Which of these two do you think went on to experience a greater seer-gifting and eventually to seeing amazing things in Heaven?

If you don't value what the Lord gives you, He is not likely to give you more. A heart of gratitude will open the storehouse of Heaven. But a heart filled with bitterness and resentment will close the window of Heaven over your spirit. When someone reports to me that they saw this beautiful cloud, I shout, "Hallelujah!" They are on their way. I get excited about what the Lord is going to show them next. Hopefully, they will pick up on the joy, excitement, and gratitude. If not, I have done my work and I leave them to the Holy Spirit.

Another interesting phenomenon I have observed is people seeing something awesome and receiving it only as something to brag about around their friends and church members. My experience has enlightened me to understand that this is why the Lord is not conducting sight-seeing tours of Heaven merely to give us bragging rights. Every vision, mental picture, and Third Heaven experience I have received was for training or to release gifts, healing, impartation, and/or words of knowledge. They are all for building us up or for the spreading of the Kingdom of God in order to bring people closer to Jesus.

I never just stop with the experience itself. I begin to pray for wisdom, revelation, counsel, understanding, might, and the fear of the Lord (Isaiah 11:2). I stand on Jesus' promise that the Holy Spirit will guide me into all truth, and I am not finished until I believe I have it. Don't stop with the experience! Let the Lord lead you deeper and deeper in wisdom and revelation! Amen!

VALUING A REBUKE

There is at least one more issue to be dealt with in this lesson. Many people are not able to receive admonishment from anyone. If the Lord admonishes them, they want to run and hide. I ask you to study and assimilate the passages below:

"Turn at my rebuke; Surely I will pour out my spirit on you; I will make my words known to you." (Proverbs 1:23)

"Because you disdained all my counsel, And would have none of my rebuke, I also will laugh at your calamity; I will mock when your terror comes." (Proverbs 1:25-26)

"They would have none of my counsel and despised my every rebuke. Therefore they shall eat the fruit of their own way, And be filled to the full with their own fancies." (Proverbs 1:30-31)

"Do not correct a scoffer, lest he hate you; Rebuke a wise man, and he will love you." (Proverbs 9:8)

"Poverty and shame will come to him who disdains correction, But he who regards a rebuke will be honored." (Proverbs 13:18)

"He who disdains instruction despises his own soul, But he who heeds rebuke gets understanding. The fear of the Lord is the instruction of wisdom, And before honor is humility." (Proverbs 15:32-33)

I value my time with the Lord so much that I do not want to get even one step off the path, because I do not want to be disqualified and out of His favor. I want to walk on the highway of holiness. I want to have clean hands and a pure heart so that I can ascend the mountain of the Lord. Therefore, I pray for discipline, rebuke, and admonishment. I want to receive it right away while it is still easy to correct and simple to get back on the path. I know very well that it is not because of my righteousness that I am allowed to visit Him. It is His righteousness and His worthiness which I am allowed to wear like a garment. But I also know clearly that willful disobedience and a rebellious spirit will block the way.

Our awesome Father God is not someone who is cold, calculating, and unfeeling or who enjoys admonishing His children. He does it because He wants what is best for us. Therefore, it is extremely important to remember that it is His love which motivates the Lord to give admonishment, correction, and an occasional rebuke. Meditate on the scripture below:

> *"My son, do not despise the chastening of the Lord, Nor detest His correction; For whom the Lord loves He corrects, Just as a father the son in whom he delights."* (Proverbs 3:11-12)

Referencing this teaching from the Proverbs, the writer of Hebrews expands on this basic and foundational truth of the gospel:

> *"And you have forgotten the exhortation which speaks to you as to sons: 'My son, do not despise the chastening of the Lord, Nor be discouraged when you are rebuked by Him; For whom the Lord loves He chastens, And scourges every son whom He receives.' If you endure chastening, God deals with you as with sons; for what son is there whom a father does not chasten? But if you are without chastening, of which all have become partakers, then you are illegitimate and not sons."* (Hebrews 12:5-8)

If you are not receiving chastening from the Lord, perhaps you need to ask yourself and the Holy Spirit why. Are we sons and daughters of the Lord or not? If we are, then the scriptures teach us that we will experience His discipline. If you are not willing to receive His loving discipline, the Holy Spirit may draw back from you. He may also release a rebuke of sufficient magnitude that you cannot ignore it any longer. I don't want this kind of rebuke. So I pray for quick discipline and to be admonished every time I need it.

If you are not yet fully able to handle a rebuke, you may need to go to the Holy Spirit school of training and discipline. This is so critical to our walk with the Lord. How can He lead us if He cannot correct us? How can we learn to follow one we don't allow to teach us, train us, correct us, and discipline us? Until we are fully open to rebuke, admonishment, and discipline, we cannot walk in the fullness of what the Lord has for us. We, in effect, temporarily disqualify ourselves from heavenly visitation.

PREPARING FOR THE LAST DAYS

"Little children, it is the last hour; and as you have heard that the Antichrist is coming, even now many antichrists have come, by which we know that it is the last hour. They went out from us, but they were not of us; for if they had been of us, they would have continued with us; but they went out that they might be made manifest, that none of them were of us." (1 John 2:18-19)

We hear often that we are living in the last days, but John's warning is more urgent. He says that this is the last hour. If it was the last hour in John's day, it must be the last five minutes now. We are living in a time of great deception, and we must learn how to test the spirits. You need to ask the Holy Spirit to give you an increase in the gift of discerning spirits. Test everything! Test this writing and see if it is in keeping with the Word of God and the witness of the Holy Spirit. We must be ready and able to hear the voice of the Lord in these critical hours. How will you be able to recognize His voice unless you hear it? How will you know the truth unless the Holy Spirit guides you? This is the time of preparation and I am convinced the Lord wants to do this work in you. I hope you will not take offense at my words. As I write this, I am convinced that if you are taking the time to read this, the following passage is about you.

> *"But you have an anointing from the Holy One, and you know all things. I have not written to you because you do not know the truth, but because you know it, and that no lie is of the truth."* (1 John 2:20-21)

HOW CAN WE LEARN TO VALUE?

Several years ago, I came to the conclusion that the key is to know the Word of God. I made a decision that I would give the first fruits of every day to the Lord. I committed to spending the first hours of every day in the Word and in worship. I paid a price for this decision, but it is something I have chosen to live by. In the military, I often had to be at work by 4 a.m. This meant I had to arise at 2:00 a.m. to give the Lord the first fruits. Often, my duties kept me up until near midnight with a 4:00 a.m. call tomorrow. I will not deceive you. The enemy tried to use my human weaknesses to get me to break my commitment to the Lord. I thank God that He gave me the strength to continue and that He provided rest to replace what I gave up for Him. He is faithful and good all the time.

It would be nice if I could say that the Lord opened the heavens to me right away. But the truth is that these experiences with the Lord began to flow after several years of paying the price. This information doesn't inspire many people to seek. But there is something very important in this testimony.

You have to value something in order to endure hardships and be willing to pay the price. Another truth is that paying the price increases the value you place on your relationship with the Lord.

In the Army, we provided training on many topics on a regular basis. I was certified in many different teaching disciplines to provide this training. During some periods of time, training money was readily available and we could provide everything at no charge to the participants. However, we quickly learned that this was a mistake. People don't value things which are free. Free books didn't get read. Free classes were not well attended. We discovered that even a very small charge for the training materials and classes produced very different results. People who paid as low as two dollars for a $20 book were more likely to read it. Why? Because they valued what they had to pay a price to receive.

I encourage you to find a way to pay a price to have your time with the Lord. Some have told me that they have to have 8-9 hours of sleep in order to function the next day and, as a result, they will have to give up their time with the Lord. I am not very impressed by these remarks, since I went for months at a time averaging two hours of sleep per night. I am not advocating this sleep pattern, but I am advocating finding a way to pay the price for what you value.

VALUING OPENS THE DOOR FOR MORE!

If you are a parent, you know this truth: You are always inspired to give more to a child who knows how to show gratitude. Gratitude is a testimony that something received is truly valued. It is a big challenge to give more to an ungrateful child. Unappreciated gifts are not used. Unappreciated gifts are thrown away or broken without cause. The giver has to pay a price for the gifts which are freely given, but not valued by the recipient. The one who pays the price values the gifts they are freely giving and the anointing they are imparting. It is not easy to keep giving to someone who does not value your gifts. Learn a lesson from this about your relationship with your heavenly Father. If you want more, then show gratitude for everything. This is the key to expanding the umbrella of God's favor over your entire life. And it is the key to receiving more spiritual gifts and more Third Heaven visits.

PRAYER

"May the Lord give you increase more and more, You and your children. May you be blessed by the Lord, Who made heaven and earth. The heaven, even the heavens, are the Lord's; But the earth He has given to the children of men." (Psalm 115:14-15)

SUMMARY

When the Lord first gave me the assignment to write this book during one of my visits to Heaven, He instructed me to impart Third Heaven visitation to others. I have done this many times since receiving that command. Over time, the manner in which I release this impartation has changed several times. Several months ago, I had a very unusual training experience in Heaven which has given this impartation what I believe to be its final form.

At the end of a training conference I was leading in Chicago, the prayer line was very long and many people came back three or four times for prayer and impartation. At about 1:00 a.m., we gathered in the meeting room just outside the pastor's office to catch our breath and review the conference. The energy level was still very high in spite of the fatigue each of us felt. The pastor received a phone call, and it was clear that it was not good news. He was conducting a two-week series of conferences in Korea and the main speaker was no longer able to travel. The conference was scheduled to occur in just a few weeks. The pastor asked if I would be willing to fill in for the other speaker. After discussing it with my wife, we shared that there were several personal reasons why we did not wish to go.

The following morning, I had a very interesting visit to the Third Heaven. I was standing under the portico of the Temple in Heaven, completely fascinated by what I was seeing. The entire exterior wall of the Temple is made of pure gold, and the pillars of the portico are also of pure gold. I was watching as the light reflected off of the pillar and back to the wall. It would then reflect back to the pillar. One important piece of information is that, in Heaven, you are not limited by the natural laws on Earth. I was able to slow the movement of the light down and literally watch the same light reflecting back and forth. I was totally caught up in this experience. Then the Lord nudged my left arm with His arm as He stepped up next to me. He was holding a calendar which He thrust in front of me and directed me to look at it very carefully. On the top of the calendar, the month and year were the same as the ministry trip to Korea. I didn't know the exact days of the month for the ministry trip, but the Lord had highlighted a two-week period in that month. I later found out that these were the exact days of the scheduled ministry trip. The Lord said that He was going to release a powerful outpouring from Heaven during that period of time and that I should not miss it. He pointed to one particular day and said that something very special and very powerful was going to be released on that day.

When I returned from my visit to Heaven, it was very clear that the Lord was telling me to go on that ministry trip. So, after discussing it with my wife, I had to humble myself and call the pastor. I was still not fully ready in my spirit to go and said, "If you can't find anyone else, I will go!" I was really hoping he had already found someone else. However, his search stopped with those words and we were committed to going on that trip. I was very excited about the Lord's promise to release something special and I looked forward to that experience.

As we prepared for the trip, I had to develop an entirely new teaching series in just a few weeks. I had agreed to use the previous speaker's topic so that the advertisements would not have to be changed. The topic was "Into Holy Spirit Fire." I liked the topic and was having a rewarding time preparing the messages. I didn't know that the Lord was also making some preparations which included providing me with some very specialized training in Heaven.

The training during my heavenly visits came in at least

two parts. Part one is what I wrote up the morning I received this teaching from the Lord. It is important to note that I was replacing a man in his thirties and I am in my sixties. The young man had offered to speak twice a day every day he was there and to be the speaker on the first day after he arrived in country. It is easier to do that when you are in your thirties. I was also in the middle of completing the final editing in order to submit two books for publication. This information will help you to understand this first part of the training in Heaven. It may also be helpful to know that this was on the morning of Shabbat.

TRAINING - PART 1

Wow! What a morning! I opened my computer and it crashed. It had been having lots of problems as I worked on the two books titled "A Warrior's Guide to the Seven Spirits of God: Part 1 (Basic Training)" and "Part 2 (Advanced Individual Training)." As I worked on the final editing, things would disappear from the screen and then reappear (at least in part), the fonts used in the text would suddenly change and then change back. Programs stopped working, etc. My computer crashed and the new router was fried. Wow! I wonder who was doing that?

I purchased a replacement computer and it arrived the day before this visit to Heaven. At last, I had it set up and had all of my information and data transferred. Isn't God good? It arrived one day before the other computer had its final crash and I had all the data backed up. Then, a few minutes later the whole cable network went down. So I fired up my Verizon hotspot so I could send the message out and it wouldn't work. I had to get it updated on-line before it would work, and I had no on-line service. The prince of the power of the air was very busy that day. But God is so much better! Amen!

On a morning like this, I saw an open Heaven. It was so beautiful. I was amazed by the many shades of blue and other colors I can't name because they are not in our natural color spectrum. The colors were so crystal clear. Then I saw the Lord standing in the opening. His appearance was awesome and power was pulsing out from Him. I expected to hear Him say, "Come up here!" But He said, "You need to spend more time with me!" I knew very well that I did need to spend more time with Him. I had spent hundreds of hours on the three books I was writing (two of them now finished) and more hours preparing for conferences, sermons, and seminars in addition to conducting training programs. I readily acknowledged that I needed to spend more time with Him. However, this message was not just for me. It is for you, too.

Then the Lord said, "You need to spend more time with me in preparation for what is about to be released! You need to spend time with me, resting up for the intensity of what is to come! You need to spend time with me to prepare to receive more. If you don't prepare now, you will have a limited experience of the outpouring in August!"

If we want what He is about to pour out, we need to get ready for it. The word came early to give us time to get ready. We need to be rested! We need to be more spiritually open in order to receive more. We need the strength, authority, and power which comes from spending time with Him. It was clear from what He said and how He said it that this was very important.

I have a difficult time resting. I love life too much to sleep very long! I love the Lord too much to wait very long to get into the Word, worship, and His presence. Perhaps you have difficulty resting, too. Then the Lord reminded me that it was Shabbot, a time for rest. So I relaxed and rested. When I did, the Lord took me on a tour of the clouds above Earth. We soared through misty clouds. It was beautiful and I felt so rested and refreshed. How many of us have difficulty just resting? We live in a high speed society which expects more and more. But without rest, we will only be able to give less and less. I pray that you will receive rest, renewal, and refreshment from the Lord as I did that morning! Amen!

TRAINING - PART 2

All I can say about this morning is WOW! As I started up the stairs to the worship room this morning, the power of God came down so heavily that I had to stop on the steps and just receive it for a while. Then I slowly made my way up the stairs as the power kept coming down. During the thanksgiving and praise time, the glory presence of the Lord kept pouring down. Face down, I sought the Lord's face and a Word from Heaven for today.

I began to see the faces of people who were crying out to be in the Lord's presence. But, as I looked into their faces, something was not quite right. The faces seemed vacant and emotionless. Then I realized that each one had on a mask covering their true self from others, but it was also blocking them from being fully in the presence of the Lord. I heard the Lord saying, "You need to remove the masks, now!" Then people began to lift their masks from the chin upward, leaving the masks on top of their heads. They had worn them a very long time as a defense mechanism and were not really ready to let them go completely. However, their desire to seek the Lord had grown stronger than their need to mask their true nature. It is useless to hide from God anyway. Here are a couple of scriptures to consider:

> *"But Jesus would not entrust himself to them, for he knew all men. He did not need man's testimony about man, for he knew what was in a man."* (John 2:24-25, NIV)

> *"At this, some of the teachers of the law said to themselves, 'This fellow is blaspheming!' Knowing their thoughts, Jesus said, 'Why do you entertain evil thoughts in your hearts?'"* (Matthew 9:3-4, NIV)

Just before this vision began I had been praying, "Lord, I am available! Use me any way you desire!" I asked for an anointing on my hands for healing and impartation of fire. Then I felt fire covering my arms and hands from my elbows down to the tips of my fingers.

I was then taken to a different place in Heaven. Jesus was standing in front of me and to my right side. In front of me, I saw a very long prayer line. My first thought was, "Why would anyone in Heaven want a prayer from me? I am still living on the Earth and they have already entered their eternity in Heaven." The Lord then told me that this was an impartation line. My first thought was, "Why would anyone in Heaven need or even want an impartation from me?" The Lord knew my thoughts and answered, "It's not for them! It's for you! I am going to teach you how to impart a renewed mind!" This was something totally new to me. I had never heard of an impartation for the renewing of the mind, and it seemed like a strange concept to me.

The Lord instructed me to lay hands on people in a way I had never used before. The palms of my hands were over their eyes with my fingers around the sides of their heads (over their ears) and both thumbs were touching the center of their foreheads. I didn't get my hands positioned correctly the first couple of times, and the Lord took my hands and formed them into the correct posture. When I did this, I felt intense power flowing from Him, through me, and into those receiving the impartation. Each time I did this, I saw the Lord Jesus put His hand on top of their heads. His hand looked like it was on fire, and I could feel the heat on my hands, which were still releasing the impartation. I knew that the important part of this was His touch and not mine. I was told to be obedient and He would do the rest. Then the Lord said, "I am releasing an anointing for the renewing of minds! I am releasing an anointing on you to pass this impartation on to others! I will renew, refine and purify the minds of those who will lift their masks and humble themselves to receive it!"

I wish I could tell you that I immediately responded with willingness to obey. However, that is not what happened. I had to go through a type of renewing of my own mind so that I would be able to be obedient to the Lord for this anointing. When I came back from Heaven, I shared this with my wife. When I finished telling her what happened, she said, "Well, your hands sort of look like a dove." I looked at my hands and agreed that they did have a shape similar to a dove, but I was fairly sure this was not what it meant. Then I admitted to her that I was struggling with the idea of offering it to people because this is a very personal way of touching people. I was unsure if anyone would really want to be touched this way. When I do this, my hands cover almost the whole face, and I had difficulty with the idea that people would want me to do that.

The Lord has been very faithful to answer my prayers for discipline and admonishment, and He answered that prayer in a very short period of time. I was back in Heaven standing in the same spot with Jesus in front and on my right side. There was the impartation line again. Coming back like this on a second visit really startled me. Then the Lord announced, "Re-training!" I was told to go back through the entire procedure. One by one, people came forward for the impartation. Each time, Jesus' hand was on their heads release a refining and purifying fire. Each time, the Lord made sure that I was holding my hands correctly. Then the Lord looked directly in my eyes and gave me a very stern order. He said, "I am telling you to do this! Do you think you can do it now?" Wow! That was a very memorable experience. I knew that there was only one correct answer. I stood at attention and said a firm "Yes, Sir! I can do that!"

At this point, I took a chance and asked the Lord a question. "If I am anointed to do this for others, who will do it for me?" I really wanted the Lord to impart this to me, but I didn't ask directly. I share this to make a point. If you want something from the Lord, ask directly! Tell Him what you want! The Lord answered my question, but not in the way I wanted. He said, "I have uniquely created you to impart this to yourself. If you will hold your hands up with your palms facing you and cross your arms, your hands will come together in the same way as when you impart to others." I did this, and it worked. So I imparted it to myself. I still longed to receive it directly from the Lord, but had to wait until November to receive it on another visit to Heaven. It came after I had been obedient to this command many times.

Near the end of the first conference in Korea, I shared this experience and command from the Lord. I was still struggling with the issue of the personal nature of this impartation and told the congregation that I would understand if they didn't want to be touched this way. I was also aware that many Korean people do not like for others to touch their heads and you need to have permission before doing this. When I invited those who would like to have this impartation to come forward, I was shocked again. It was like a stampede. Everyone came running forward and I was almost knocked over from the rush. I was the speaker for several conferences back to back for two weeks and had the same response from every different congregation.

After giving this impartation at the last church conference on this ministry trip, a very good Korean friend of mine—who also happens to be a Torah scholar—came up and asked, "Do you know what that is?" As he asked this, he had his hands together the way Jesus had taught me. I admitted that I didn't fully understand it, but was being obedient to the Lord. He said, "This is the Aaronic blessing. This is how Aaron held his hands while blessing the people. It forms the Hebrew letter 'shin' which looks similar to a letter 'w' in English. It has two very powerful meanings. It stands for the name of God and fire." Wow! This really caught my interest and initiated an extensive search for the full meaning of this Hebrew blessing.

As I studied from several Hebrew websites and various scholars, I came to understand that this Hebrew character has four primary meanings, all of which directly relate to imparting a renewed mind.

1. It is the primary character in the word "Shaddai"—God Almighty or God of the Mountains (See Genesis 17:1, Psalm 68:14, 91:1). This word derives from the root word "shadad" which means to destroy or to completely overpower.

2. It is the primary character in the word "esh" or Fire. The Hebrew character "shin" is often written with flames coming from all three upper points of the letter. Another interesting and powerful idea is that it is always related to the Hebrew word "iysh" meaning man. (See Ezekiel 10:6-7)

3. It is the primary character in the Hebrew word "shoov" meaning repent in the sense of having a complete change of thinking.

4. It is the primary character in the Hebrew word "shalom" meaning peace, wholeness and wellness.

This study led me to the Aaronic blessing given in the sixth chapter of the book of Numbers. This resulted in another huge revelation. The Complete Jewish Bible makes the meaning of this passage even more clear:

"Adonai said to Moshe, 'Speak to Aharon and his sons, and tell them that this is how you are to bless the people of Isra'el: you are to say to them,

'Y'varekh'kha Adonai v'yishmerekha,

[May Adonai bless you and keep you.]

Ya'er Adonai panav eleikha vichunekka.

[May Adonai make his face shine on you and show you his favor.]

Yissa Adonai panav eleikha v'yasem l'kha sha-lom.

[May Adonai lift up his face toward you and give you peace.]'"

(Numbers 6:22-26, CJB)

I was stunned when I considered verse 27 in this translation:

"In this way they are to put my name on the people of Isra'el, so that I will bless them."
(Numbers 6:27, CJB)

After seeing this clearly for the first time, I went to Ezekiel, Chapter 9:

"Now the glory of the God of Israel had gone up from the cherub, where it had been, to the threshold of the temple. And He called to the man clothed with linen, who had the writer's ink-horn at his side; and the Lord said to him, 'Go through the midst of the city, through the midst of

Jerusalem, and put a mark on the foreheads of the men who sigh and cry over all the abominations that are done within it.'" (Ezekiel 9:3-4)

I received by revelation that the man clothed in linen will place the Hebrew character "shin" on the foreheads of all those whose hearts are aligned with Father God's heart. Part of this revelation came during that August trip to Korea. In one location, I had a strange experience at breakfast the morning I planned to release this impartation during the evening service. I began to feel a very strong pulse in my thumbs. This was strange and I couldn't remember ever feeling this before and commented to my wife about it. I said, "I can feel my pulse in my thumbs! I never felt that before!" As quickly as this came out of my mouth, I heard the Lord say, "That's not your pulse! It's mine! When you impart to people, you are putting my heartbeat into them and their hearts will begin to come into synchronization with my heartbeat! They will begin to love what I love and care about the things which I value!" Wow! This was getting deeper and deeper! Then the Lord led me one step further. I was guided to the passage below from the book of Revelation:

"Then I saw another angel ascending from the east, having the seal of the living God. And he cried with a loud voice to the four angels to whom it was granted to harm the earth and the sea, saying, 'Do not harm the earth, the sea, or the trees till we have sealed the servants of our God on their foreheads.' And I heard the number of those who were sealed. One hundred and forty-four thousand of all the tribes of the children of Israel were sealed:" (Revelation 7:2-4)

By revelation from the Holy Spirit, I came to understand that the mark on their foreheads will be the same Hebrew character "shin." Now I understood more fully what Numbers 6:27 was referring to. This impartation was putting the seal of God on people when they truly allowed Jesus to renew their minds with His fiery hand. This was literally putting the name of God, "Shaddai," on the foreheads of His people.

When the Lord first commanded me to release this impartation, I was completely unaware of its meaning. I had never seen or heard of any of this. Now it was becoming an increasingly and extremely precious anointing to me.

AN IMPARTATION

To impart this to yourself, simply lift your hands up in front of your face with your palms facing toward you. Cross your hands so that they come together as in the figure above. Place your hands with your palms over your eyes, your fingers toward or over your ears and with your thumbs on your forehead. Remember it is not about what is in your hands. It is about obedience and about the hand of Jesus.

Now, speak the words of the Aaronic blessing over yourself. I have paraphrased it below so that you can speak it over yourself in the first person. As you speak the words, begin to sense the fiery hand of Jesus on your head. As you feel the heat from His fiery hand on the top of your head, you will come to the assurance that this impartation is truly being given to you by *Yeshua ha Messiach.*

"The Lord bless me and keep me;
The Lord make His face shine upon me, And be gracious to me;

The Lord lift up His countenance upon me, And give me peace.

So I shall put the Lord's name on my forehead, and He will bless me."

(Numbers 6:24-27, paraphrased)

In addition to the blessing, I always proclaim something like the following:

"Begin to feel the fiery hand of Jesus on your head. I decree that your spiritual eyes are being opened wide so that your seer anointing will increase and you can begin to see into the Third Heaven. Your spiritual ears are being opened fully so that you can hear the voice of the Lord speaking to you. Begin to hear Him say, 'Come up here!'" I impart to you the heartbeat of the Lord so that your heart will come into sync with His, and you will begin to love what He loves and value what He values. Feel the fire as the Lord refines and purifies your mind."

I do this daily because I am convinced that this is a key to being able to visit in the Third Heaven. We have so many doctrines of man and so much of the spirit of religion in us that doubt will come back over and over unless we take steps every day to stand in faith to receive the Lord's promises. Remember what Paul said:

> "*I beseech you therefore, brethren, by the mercies of God, that you present your bodies a living sacrifice, holy, acceptable to God, which is your reasonable service. And do not be conformed to this world, but be transformed by the renewing of your mind, that you may prove what is that good and acceptable and perfect will of God.*" (Romans 12:1-2)

Stand in faith that the work which the Lord began in you will be completed. Read again (aloud if possible) Peter's description of what happened on the day of Pentecost and make it yours. Renew your mind over and over until you know with certainty that you have been anointed to see visions, speak prophetic words, and visit the Third Heaven often. Amen!

"But Peter, standing up with the eleven, raised his voice and said to them, 'Men of Judea and all who dwell in Jerusalem, let this be known to you, and heed my words. For these are not drunk, as you suppose, since it is only the third hour of the day. But this is what was spoken by the prophet Joel: "And it shall come to pass in the last days, says God, that I will pour out of My Spirit on all flesh; Your sons and your daughters shall prophesy, Your young men shall see visions, Your old men shall dream dreams. And on My menservants and on My maidservants I will pour out My Spirit in those days; And they shall prophesy. I will show wonders in Heaven above and signs in the earth beneath: Blood and fire and vapor of smoke. The sun shall be turned into darkness, and the moon into blood, before the coming of the great and awesome day of the Lord. And it shall come to pass that whoever calls on the name of the Lord shall be saved."'" (Acts 2:14-21)

Throughout the scriptures, God has been very clear about His intentions. In the last days, He plans to pour out His Spirit on all flesh. In this outpouring, it should be the norm that His modern-day disciples experience and report visions, dreams, and words of prophecy. The fulfillment of this prophecy is rarely seen in denominational churches today. Those who have visions and give words of prophecy have been at best marginalized and at worst called heretics by members of the mainstream churches. Some teach that the dispensation, prophesied by Joel and explained by Peter, has come and gone.

The absence of visions, dreams, and prophecies in the church is tragic. How will we hear from the Lord except by the methods He has established? Is He known only in the scriptures or do we have a personal God who interacts with His people?

Has God left us to our own programs, designs, and visions or is He still in charge; leading His people with a cloud by day and a column of fire at night?

On the other hand, many of those who have developed an intense desire for the fulfillment of this prophesy have found themselves running from prophet to prophet, visionary to visionary, and dreamer to dreamer seeking to hear the Word of God. In each conference or sermon, they hear a Word, pick up some new vocabulary, and become like parrots. They are merely repeating the words given to another. At best they become pale shadows of the latest movement.

I believe that, in these last days, God is calling all believers to come forth and receive the messages of the kingdom directly from Him.

> *"But the anointing which you have received from Him abides in you, and you do not need that anyone teach you; but as the same anointing teaches you concerning all things, and is true, and is not a lie, and just as it has taught you, you will abide in Him."* (1 John 2:27)

If you have difficulty staying focused during this experience, try praying James 4:7. I turned the truth of this passage into a prayer to prevent distractions from blocking me and to set myself free from any demonic oppression during my time with the Lord.

PRAYER

"Father God, I submit to you in spirit, soul, and body: all that I am and all that I will ever be; all that I have and all that I will ever have, I submit to you. I resist the devil! In accordance with your Word and in the mighty name of Jesus, he must flee and take all his works with him, in Jesus' name! Amen and Amen!"

POINTS TO PONDER

Be a prophet and not a parrot.

- Parrots repeat what they hear from others. They often get only part of it because it isn't their revelation.
- Prophets bring the Word directly from Heaven. It is then first-hand information.

Learn to value sharing your experiences and allow yourself to learn from the experiences of others.

> *"As iron sharpens iron, so one man sharpens another."* (Proverbs 27:17, NIV)

- Who is being sharpened by the iron in your testimony?
- Whose testimony is sharpening the iron in your spirit and soul?

> *"Deep calls to deep in the roar of your waterfalls; all your waves and breakers have swept over me."* (Psalm 42:7, NIV)

And finally: Trust God to provide what you need to know. What can you do?

- Be Holy Spirit directed
- Be Holy Spirit taught
- Be Holy Spirit equipped
- Be Holy Spirit protected
- Be Holy Spirit provided
- Stop chasing after the latest wind of doctrine
- Chase after fresh revelation from Heaven
- Seek what Heaven is saying today

OTHER BOOKS BY THIS AUTHOR:

"A Warrior's Guide to the Seven Spirits of God" - Part 1: Basic Training, by James A. Durham, Copyright © James A. Durham, printed by Xulon Press, August 2011.

"A Warrior's Guide to the Seven Spirits of God" - Part 2: Advanced Individual Training, by James A. Durham, Copyright © James A. Durham, printed by Xulon Press, August 2011.

CPSIA information can be obtained at www.ICGtesting.com
Printed in the USA
LVOW13s1054080913

351492LV00002B/438/P